The Well Digger
Copyright © 2020 F. Lionel Young III
Published in Austin, Texas (USA) by Desert Creek

All rights reserved. No part of this publication may be reproduced, distributed, or transmitted in any form or by any means, including photocopying, recording, or other electronic or mechanical methods, without the prior written permission of the publisher.

Young, F. Lionel III (Fleetwood Lionel) 1967–
    The well digger: flourishing in your desert /
        by F. Lionel Young III.
    Includes references and bibliography.

ISBN: 978-0-578-77547-0 (paperback)

Library of Congress Control Number: 2020919144

Book design by Baily Bada
Edited by Sarah White
Cover image by Getty Images

Formatting for electronic versions may vary by device.

Unless otherwise noted, Scripture citations are from THE HOLY BIBLE, NEW INTERNATIONAL VERSON® NIV® Copyright © 1973, 1978, 1984 by International Bible Society® Used by permission. All rights reserved worldwide.

Author bio and contact information can be found inside the back cover.

In loving memory of my grandfather
Ennis Isaac Davis (1910–1988)

THE
WELL
DIGGER

F. Lionel Young III

Desert Creek | Austin, Texas

"Your task is to dig wells in your desert."
—Eugene Peterson

Contents

Introduction

This is a little book about flourishing in the desert in the middle of a famine. It is written to be an encouragement to anyone who has faced disappointing loss. It is the story of Isaac, the forgotten patriarch. He faced famine, failure (his own), frustration and foe—and he never gave up. He just kept digging wells, and God continued to bless him everywhere he moved. This book is a reflection on Genesis 26, a spiritual exposition intended to encourage the followers of Christ to "wait for the Lord, be strong, and take heart." The aim is to strengthen readers to "remain confident" that in due time, they will "see the goodness of the Lord."[1]

The New Testament writers show us how to read the Old Testament stories—the true tales that were written down before the arrival of the Messiah about our "ancestors." Paul tells us that they followed "Christ" in the desert, though they did not see him as clearly as we do now. The stories from the Torah were "written down as warnings" and "examples" for us today.[2] The accounts of ancients like Abraham, Isaac and Jacob, as well as the biographical sketches of people like Moses, Rahab, Gideon and Samson, were written to encourage

---

[1] Ps. 27:13–14.

[2] I Cor. 10:1–13.

us to persevere in our faith with the unflagging confidence that God does reward those who diligently seek him.[3] The stories found in Scripture were written for our encouragement and instruction.[4] Isaac's story is for us today.

A Personal Journey

This little book came out of a season of reflection on my own journey. It has been my custom to read through the entirety of the Scriptures each year of my life since I was a young teenager. This repetitious reading of the text may sound monotonous, but the effect has given me a profound appreciation for the richness of God's word. Earlier this year, I was struck by the story of Isaac in Genesis 26, and it became a constant source of meditation over the course of several months. I couldn't stop thinking about this text, and I couldn't stop talking to my family about it. I decided to dig a little deeper, and I discovered a fountain that has refreshed my soul. Honestly, I never intended that these thoughts would become a book. I had just finished meeting a writing deadline for an academic work that was mentally exhausting, and I was ready for a reprieve. In a way, writing this little book was the break I needed from writing! I simply took many of the thoughts from

---

[3] Heb. 11:1—12:3.

[4] George W. Knight III, "The Scriptures Were Written for Our Instruction," *Journal of the Evangelical Theological Society*, Vol. 39, No. 1 (March 1996): 3–13.

my reading and reflection and wrote them down over the course of a few weeks.

I have shared a few confessions from my own life in this little manuscript (though none as transparent as Augustine's!). Everyone experiences setbacks and suffering in this life, and I have learned that it is rarely helpful for us to make comparisons. We do not comfort our fellow pilgrims during their time of mourning by telling them an even sadder tale about our own experience. Jesus suffered more than all of us, and yet he never minimizes our suffering. On the contrary, he listens to us and empathizes with us in our weaknesses. He encourages us to bring everything to him, asking him for grace and mercy in our time of need. Because he suffered so much, he is able to understand our lesser sufferings.[5] I cannot even begin to compare my own losses with the many stories I have heard from my brothers and sisters in Christ. I've been especially moved by the difficulties of my friends living in the non-Western world during COVID-19. Like everyone else, I have been affected by the coronavirus pandemic, but not to the extent of the people who live in places of extreme deprivation. I've had to work a lot harder during the pandemic. I have missed going to baseball games, theological libraries and some of my favorite museums. I had to cancel my annual study leave in Cambridge. What suffering I have endured! But before COVID-19 came and upended all our lives, I was still

---

[5] Heb. 11:15–16.

working through some pain and suffering of my own. We have all lost something in this world. And so some of what I write here in these pages comes out of the work the Spirit of God did in my own heart during a season of unwelcome loss. It is my prayer that those who have faced even greater pain and suffering will be blessed by these words.

Notes and Acknowledgements

For nearly thirty years, my weekly practice as a pastor involved reading Greek, Hebrew and the best commentaries and theological works I could find. I devoted my life to teaching through the Scriptures, usually entire books of the Bible, verse-by-verse-by-verse, week after week after week. This book makes use of the classical education I enjoyed in languages and theology and draws from primary sources (the text) supported by many helpful secondary sources (commentaries, theological works, journal articles, etc.). The primary source for this study is the *Biblica Hebraica Stuttgartensia* (BHS), the most widely used edition of the Hebrew Bible for students and scholars. English quotations of the Bible are from the *New International Version,* and references are footnoted to smooth out the reading. The definition of Hebrew words and phrases relies on the original work of the father of modern Hebrew, Wilhelm Gesenius (1786–1842), now edited and published under the names Brown, Driver and Briggs. I have drawn from a variety of commentaries, including works by Gordon J. Wenham, Victor P.

Hamilton, Bruce K. Waltke, Derek Kidner, Bill T. Arnold, John Calvin, James Montgomery Boice, John J. Davis, Joyce G. Baldwin and others. Shaul Bar's recent scholarly monograph on the life of Isaac is the only book-length biography of the patriarch, and I have benefited from it. Some of these works are cited in the footnotes, though I have refrained from the kind of pedantic source citation found in academic monographs. Instead, I have used references here and there for the most salient points. I have rounded out this study by relying on a variety of academic journal articles, theological dictionaries, older commentaries and a few quotes from some of my favorite people, like Augustine and Lewis. On interpretive method I side with those scholars who labor to uncover the authorial intent of the text for the original audience. In addition, I have used this story as an extended metaphor, not to change the original meaning, but to apply the original meaning to our own lives. This is how the original audience would have intuitively listened to the Book of Moses. [6] A full list of works cited is included in the bibliography.

I would like to thank my oldest son Fleetwood Young IV, who encouraged me to write this little book and also provided significant technical assistance so that we could get it out as quickly as possible. We decided to

---

[6] On this topic of how oral cultures listened to stories, see John H. Walton and D. Brent Sandy, *The Lost World of Scripture: Ancient Literary Culture and Biblical Authority* (Downers Grove, IL: IVP Academic, 2013).

avoid the traditional publishing route, not out of necessity, but because we wanted to work on a fun project together. My colleague Bailey Bada, a linguist and bibliophile, did the artwork and designed the covers. Even during COVID-19, the librarians at the Cambridge University Library worked to make it possible for students and members of the university to access a wide range of journal articles and theological resources while working from home. I would also like to thank Sarah White, a Research Fellow at the University of St Andrews, for her keen editorial skills. Many people have helped make this book better, though I bear full responsibility for any shortcomings. Finally, I would like to thank my wife for working by my side "digging wells" for more than 30 years.

1

The Famine

Now there was famine in the land — besides the previous famine in Abraham's time — and Isaac went to Abimelek king of the Philistines.
—Genesis 26:1a

I'm writing this book in the middle of a pandemic, as I hear stories about famine in some parts of the world. I work with an organization that provides theological education for underserved leaders in the developing world, and the people we serve have been profoundly impacted by the recent global crisis. The pandemic has closed many national borders, cutting off supply chains and creating food shortages. The disruption of the travel industry has affected millions of jobs, hitting people especially hard in the least developed countries (LDCs), where low-wage workers are heavily dependent on tourism. A recent study published by researchers at the Oxford Poverty & Human Development Initiative is now projecting that COVID-19 could turn back the clock on the economic progress made by developing nations by some ten years in the poorest regions of the world.[7] Americans and Europeans are certainly feeling

---

[7] S. Alkire, R. Nogales, N. N. Quinn and N. Suppa, "On Track or Not? Projecting the Global Multidemensional

the effects of COVID-19, but the developing world will be hit much harder. A July Oxfam study is now forecasting that more people will die from starvation in 2020 than from the disease itself.[8] We are living through a modern-day famine.

Famines have been around a long time. They frequently occurred in the ancient world and sometimes lasted for several years.[9] One of the most well-known famines in the Bible occurred during the life of Joseph, the son of Jacob, although famines also occurred during the days of Abraham and Isaac. Food shortages were usually associated with abnormally low rainfall, and water was a valuable commodity in the semi-arid regions of the world we often refer to as the Middle East. Most of us who live in the North Atlantic West (those most likely to read this book) have reliable access to food, water, health care and other basic necessities, unlike many of our neighbors in the Southern hemispheres. While I was in a staff meeting with our team from many parts of the world during the early weeks of COVID-19, our differences became even more apparent during a rather comical exchange. Our

---

Poverty Index," OPHI Research in Progress, 58a (University of Oxford, 2020).

[8] Oxfam Media Briefing, "The Hunger Virus: How COVID-19 is Fuelling Hunger in a Hungry World," July 9, 2020: https://oxfamilibrary.openrepository.com/bitstream/handle/10546/621023/mb-the-hunger-virus-090720-en.pdf.

[9] Bill T. Arnold, *Genesis* (Cambridge, UK: Cambridge University Press, 2014), 239.

directors in India and Cuba wanted to know why a possible toilet paper shortage was making headlines in North America! As you can imagine, the bathroom humor was not in short supply during that staff meeting. It was good to laugh, even as we were reminded of how different life can be depending on where you live in the world.

North Americans and Western Europeans live very different lives from their brothers and sisters in the developing world. Still, every son and daughter of Abraham has experienced periods of deprivation in one form or another. Some of you reading this book have been through unspeakable losses, times that make you feel like a person wandering alone through a desert wasteland in the middle of a famine. Privation can come in so many different ways in this life. The unexpected loss of a job, the discouraging closure of a business, the heart-sickening end to a cherished friendship, the painful death of a family member, a divorce that leaves you curled up in the fetal position, an injury that ends a promising athletic career—or a thousand other things that make you just want to stop living. If others minimize your loss, know that Jesus doesn't. I'm thinking of people I love as I write these words—family members, friends and co-workers. May this story encourage us all to persevere with unshakeable hope in the goodness of God.

The Forgotten Patriarch

Everyone knows about Abraham, the father of many nations and the friend of God. He is the celebrated patron of the Jewish people and the forefather of every follower of Christ. He trusted God and was justified (made righteous) before the law of Moses was even given. This is why Paul cleverly uses Abraham to argue with legalists that we are saved by grace without the law. Abraham is "the father of all who believe."[10] He is the inspiration for the rest of us to persevere in faith, to continue "longing for a better country—a heavenly one."[11] We are also familiar with the stories of Jacob, Abraham's grandson—the one whose name was changed to Israel. His name, before it was changed to Israel, meant "to supplant" or "overthrow." In contemporary English, his name would be rendered, "someone who attacks from behind in order to get ahead."[12] The story of Jacob's Ladder and that strange account of the time when he wrestled with God have been enshrined in the Western mind by celebrated artists like William Blake (1757–1827) and Eugène Delacroix (1798–1863). Tourists to the Holy Land often visit Jacob's Well, located inside the walls of an ancient monastery in Israel. This sacred site has been associated with the eponymous patriarch for more than two thousand years. [13] Isaac, the son of Abraham and father of Jacob, is often passed over in the patriarchal

---

[10] Rom. 4:11.

[11] Heb. 11:16.

[12] Francis Brown, S. R. Driver and Charles A. Briggs, *A Hebrew and English Lexicon of the Old Testament* (Oxford, UK: Oxford University Press, 1951), 784–5.

[13] W. Ewing and D. J. Wend, "Jacob's Well," in *The International Bible Encyclopedia*, ed. Geoffrey W. Bromiley (Grand Rapids, MI: Eerdmans, 1982), 955.

narratives. He's the forgotten patriarch. He doesn't even have a famous well named after him, even though digging wells is the one thing for which he is most famous. Only recently has a book-length study been published on Isaac's life. The Jewish scholar Shaul Bar observes in the introduction to his work on the patriarch: "Surprisingly, there has not been a single comprehensive book about Isaac's entire life written so far, only those devoted to his binding story."[14] His story has been largely glossed over.

There is one entire chapter in the Bible that is devoted to Isaac's life: Genesis 26. The chapter serves as an important bridge between Abraham and Isaac.[15] The story of Isaac shows how the blessing of God that began with his promise to Abraham is handed down to his son. Set within the larger story of the biblical narrative, it is a story of God's faithfulness to keep his promises to every generation that believes. The story of Isaac is the narrative of a flawed person who faced one setback after another, but he never lost faith. He encountered famine, failure, frustration and foe. But he just kept digging wells in the deserts of Palestine. And the Well Digger prospered.

On the Causes of Famines

One of the most difficult things about famines in the ancient world was that there truly was nothing you

[14] Shaul Bar, *Isaac: The Passive Patriarch* (Eugene, OR: Wipf & Stock, 2019), 229, Kindle.

[15] Victor P. Hamilton, *The Book of Genesis, Chapters 18–50* (Grand Rapids, MI: Eerdmans, 1995), 190.

could do to prevent them. Famines just showed up and made life hard for everyone. Genesis 26 begins with an opening line that is theologically unremarkable: "Now there was a famine in the land." We are not told much else. There is no further commentary. We are not told why. Much like our modern-day pandemic, seasons of deprivation in ancient Palestine[16] often came without a word from God. The strange days of lockdowns and quarantines and travel bans have reminded all of us that we don't have as many answers as we thought we did, and we are not the masters of our own fate.

It doesn't matter how wise or smart or godly or experienced we are—bad things are going to happen to us in this world. Yes, as people created in the *imago Dei*, we have been given the task of ruling over creation for our good and the glory of God.[17] We should continue to harness all of our God-given creativity to rule over creation and to make this world a better place. In the Judeo-Christian tradition, this is often called the Creation Mandate or the Cultural Mandate.[18] God has

---

[16] I am using the word Palestine, not in the political sense, but in reference to the geographic regions that now encompass modern-day Israel, the Palestinian Territories, Western Jordan, Lebanon and parts of Syria. I will also use the word Canaan as a synonym.

[17] Gen. 1:26–28.

[18] The Cultural Mandate is espoused most clearly within Judaism, Eastern Orthodoxy and the Protestant Reformed tradition. For an easy-to-read introduction to this doctrine, see William Edgar, "The Creation Mandate," *The Gospel Coalition*, August 25, 2020,

endowed us with creative abilities as his image-bearers and given us the task of exploring the earth, taming creation and exercising dominion over all that he has made. There is, therefore, much we can and should do to understand how this world works. But we will never be God, and the subsequent fall that occurred after God told man to rule over the world has made the human task of ruling over creation even more difficult. However, we can still flourish. We can still earn bread even if it means doing so by the sweat of our brow.[19] We can still dig wells when famines come, and we can still find water in the desert. But we cannot live under the illusion that we are able to prevent everything or control everything. Famine, injustice and adversity come into every life. Just as the "famine" came "in the days of Abraham," it also came in the days of Isaac. Sometimes there is nothing one can do to prevent it.

Isaac certainly had nothing to do with the famine, nor is he blamed for many of the things that befall him in our story. It is interesting that in this passage, the biblical writer never draws a connecting line between Isaac's flaws as a person and the frustrations he encounters in his life as a follower of God. There is no direct correlation between Isaac's sins and his setbacks. There is silence on the cause of the famine and no obvious link between Isaac's duplicitous dealings with Abimelech and the injustice and opposition he endured

---

https://www.thegospelcoalition.org/essay/the-creation-mandate/.

[19] Gen. 3:19.

13

during his wanderings in Canaan. We may make our own inferences, but we would only be guessing. On the contrary, as we will see below, Isaac continues to flourish in the face of famine and foe despite his obvious faults and failures as a follower of Yahweh.[20] There is encouragement here for every sinner—and we will talk more about this in chapter three. But this passage provides very little help on "the causes of famines"—or what theologians and philosophers call the problem of evil and suffering in this world. In order to address this larger, more complex question, we have to take a step back from Isaac's story and turn to the larger biblical narrative.

Miserable Comforters

In Albert Camus' 1948 novel *The Plague*, a deadly outbreak sweeps through the city of Oran in French Algeria. Camus' work is a vivid psychological study of the human response to a deadly epidemic. It is also a provocative reflection on the search for meaning amid suffering. One of the central characters in *The Plague* is a priest named Father Paneloux who provides spiritual leadership for the city. His character also serves as a clever theological mouthpiece for Camus (an avowed atheist). As the plague ravishes the city, the people of Oran flock to the cathedral in search of answers. Father Paneloux is well prepared his sermon on this momentous occasion. He rises for the homily, grips the

---

[20] Gordon Wenham, *Word Biblical Commentary, Genesis 16–50* (Nashville, TN: Thomas Nelson Publishers, 1994), 194–7.

wooden pulpit with his large hands, and launches into his sermon. "Calamity has come on you, my brethren, and, my brethren, you deserve it."[21] Personal sin is the lens through which some people see every sickness and setback in this life. It is the cause of everything that has come upon us, and this is frequently the first place people turn when anything bad happens to them or others. Calamity has come upon us—and we deserve it! This simplistic explanation is enticing in part because it's so easy. Sin can be found everywhere. It is ubiquitous. It fills this world.

But the most important book in the Bible on human suffering, possibly written around the time Abraham, Isaac and Jacob roamed these lands, actually pushes back hard against this oversimplification. When Job lost everything, his friends came and wept with him. When we read the story, we are immediately impressed by their compassion. But then they begin to offer explanations that Job cannot accept. The omniscient narrator lets Bildad, Eliphaz and Zophar talk.[22] They drone on and on, *ad infinitum, ad nauseam.* The point of this tedious back and forth is to show the exhausting futility of their arguments. They trot out some of the best explanations for Job's loss, and they still get it all wrong. They were not only bad theologians; they were

---

[21] Albert Camus, *The Plague* (New York, NY: Vintage, 1991), 94.

[22] The many references in Job, including the names of his friends and the places where they are from, have led scholars to argue that this work tells a story that is as old as the patriarchs themselves.

also "miserable comforters."[23] Their counsel covered the philosophical gamut, but they kept coming back to their main argument: "Submit to God and be at peace with him; in this way, prosperity will come to you."[24] Calamity had come upon Job, and he deserved it.

The problem was certainly obvious to Job's friends. This person who had been so blessed by God simply needed to get the sin out of his life—"to remove wickedness far from [his] tent." He had sinned, and he was hiding it somewhere! [25] Job was simply proud, unwilling to admit his contribution to his own calamity. If he would just come clean and confess his sin, everything would be made whole again. Righteousness would have kept the Sabeans from raiding and prevented the fire of God from falling. Holiness would have protected Job's flocks from the cruel Chaldeans and guarded his children against the great wind that took their lives. It was quite simple.

Those who preach the flawed theology of Father Paneloux and Job's friends, whether from the pulpit or the pew, are usually convinced they are right. It makes so much sense. Think about it. You don't have to look very hard to find sin—in your own life or in anyone else's. It's too easy to approach soul care like some childhood game of Connect the Dots; find the sin, find the solution! But we all know from hard experience that it's just not that simple. Still, people do it all the time. I

[23] Job 16:2.

[24] Job 22:21.

[25] Job 22:23.

have done it as a pastor, and I'm deeply grieved over the pain I unwittingly caused my "patients" in my earliest years of caring for souls. May God forgive me! It's interesting, I think, that God never told Job or his friends about what was really going on behind the scenes. He just rebuked all of them, Job included, for their lousy answers. There was nothing Job could have done to prevent his loss. Nothing. The fact is, as we all know, sometimes people suffer for doing the *right* thing. Job was singled out by Satan *because* of his piety. Connect those dots, Bildad! The truth is that personal sin is only one of many possible explanations for painful losses that come into our lives. They are probably only part of the mix. Sometimes it is best to say we don't know because that is the truth.

This does not mean that seasons of deprivation and difficulty are random. There is mystery in this life, but God is still the Author of the mystery. He is, to borrow from G. K. Chesterton, "the Storyteller."[26] And he knows how to spin a good yarn! The God of Abraham, Isaac and Jacob is sovereign over all things—even over famines and pandemics and the unexplained seasons of loss. As Bruce Waltke remarks in his commentary on this passage: "As was seen in the life of Abraham, there are famines in the ambiguities and hard reality of God's providence."[27] There is ambiguity—mystery. There are hard realities—famines and foes. Yet, in all of these

---

[26] G. K. Chesterton, *Orthodoxy* (London, UK: John Lane, 1908), 110.

[27] Bruce Waltke, *Genesis: A Commentary* (Grand Rapids, MI: Zondervan, 2001), 367.

things, we maintain our faith in the providence of God. As the followers of Christ, we express this confidence when we recite *The Apostle's Creed*: "I believe in God, the Father almighty, creator of heaven and earth." He is our Father, he is the almighty, and he is the maker and sovereign of all things in heaven, as well as the earth. As the preacher of providence, John Calvin (1509–1564), put it some five hundred years ago, the comfort of those who place their trust in God is to know that he rules all things by his wisdom:

> His solace, I say, is to know that his Heavenly Father so holds all things in his power, so rules by his authority and will, so governs by his wisdom, that nothing can befall [him] except he determine it. Moreover, it comforts him to know that he has been received into Gods' safekeeping and entrusted to the care of his angels, and that neither water, nor fire, nor iron can harm him, except in so far as it please God as governor to give them occasions.[28]

I am not comforted by faith in a God who loves me but cannot keep me. I find very little hope in a worldview that posits a present and future where things are up for grabs. We are tacitly confessing our belief in God's mysterious providence when we pray the Lord's Prayer: "Your will be done, on earth as it is in heaven."[29] The God who reigns in heaven cares about

---

[28] John Calvin, *Institutes of the Christian Religion*, in *The Library of Christian Classics*, Vol. 20, ed. John T. McNeill (Philadelphia, PA: The Westminster Press, 1960), 224.

[29] Matt. 6:10.

what happens in my life on this earth. He reigns in heaven and rules over the earth. His sovereignty is not confined to the throne room of heaven but flows from his throne to every corner of the universe. He is even, in a most mysterious way, sovereign over Satan. Job had no explanation for what happened to him, yet he bowed in painful worship and said, "The Lord gave, and the Lord has taken away."[30] God allows famine, frustration and foe to "befall" us. God offers Isaac no explanation for the famine he endured or the frustrations he encountered, one right after another. We are only told that this persistent patriarch somehow trusted God.

The Search for Answers

It is not wrong to search for answers in this mysterious world. It is normal to ask "why" in times of suffering. Why did my company fail? Why did my friend die? Why did I lose my job? Why did my wife leave me? Why did my business partner betray me? I'm one of those seekers that prefer full explanations. I'll take partial explanations—but I like answers. My inquisitive demands, however, can lead to even more frustration. Sometimes God is silent, even hidden. The old theologians of the Church had a Latin expression for it—*Deus absconditus*—"the hidden God." The precise phraseology comes from Isaiah 45:15, "Truly you are a God who has been hiding himself."[31] There are times

---

[30] Job 1:21.

[31] Isaiah 45:15. The Latin translation of the Hebrew is literally, "Deus absconditus."

when it feels like God has hidden himself, just as he did in the story of Job. There are times when he plays his cards close to his chest. Still, we try to get God to show his hand. We are usually motivated by a desire to prevent the same thing from happening again. But this too is naïve. Isaac endured repeated, similar setbacks, and there was very little he could have done to prevent it. He didn't prosper by trying to make sense of everything but by faithfully trusting God wherever he went. He was resilient. He just kept digging wells in faith.

The Scriptures do offer some wisdom in our quest for answers. But it's not as simple as we would like to think. Ancient philosophers and Christian theologians have been trying to find satisfying answers to the problem of evil for thousands of years. [32] There are many possibilities. Sometimes painful loss comes into our lives because of Satan. Once again, the story of Job is one of the clearest illustrations of this. Satan was the one behind it all, though his machinations were largely hidden from view. Job's servants, Job's wife, Job's friends, and even Job himself didn't know what actually went on in those closed-door meetings between Lucifer and Yahweh. Job's servants saw the Sabeans plundering. They felt the heat of the fire of God falling from the sky. They bore witness to the Chaldean raids. They watched as a fierce wind tore through the home of Job's children. But they never mentioned the damn

---

[32] J. S. Feinberg, "Evil, Problem of," in *Evangelical Dictionary of Theology*, ed. Walter E. Elwell (Grand Rapids, MI: Baker, 1984), 385–8.

devil. He was hidden from view.[33] The devil doesn't appear in the story of Isaac, nor do we see him prowling about in our own lives. That is because he often lurks in the shadows. That is why we pray in the Lord's Prayer, "Deliver us from the evil one."[34]

Sometimes we can blame our suffering and setbacks on others. The sins of Ahab and Jezebel brought famine on the land of Israel and everyone else, including the prophets of God.[35] There is no question, as the murder of Abel teaches us, that people can inflict murderous pain on their "brothers" because of the sin in their own hearts. [36] At times, it is unintentional (though still painful), while at other times, people actually do mean to hurt us. The story of Joseph shows us that people hatch plans against us that can change the entire trajectory of our lives.[37] Isaac, as we will see, repeatedly endured mistreatment by people who were afraid and jealous.

What often goes unnoticed in highly individualized societies (like the United States) is the nature of community sin, or what has been referred to in the Christian tradition as corporate sin. I have sometimes heard people justify certain actions by appealing to the approval of a larger group. This completely ignores the possibility that large groups of people often do get it

[33] Job 1:1–22.

[34] Matt. 6:13.

[35] 1 Kings 18.

[36] Gen. 4:2–8.

[37] Gen. 50:20.

wrong. There are many examples of this in Scripture, as well as in our modern world. There was "outcry" over the systemic sins of Sodom and Gomorrah.[38] Joseph's brothers were united in their plot against him, and all except one sibling agreed to cause him bodily harm.[39] An Egyptian king used the power of his government to force the Israelites to become slave laborers.[40] More than 250 community leaders started a campaign to overthrow Moses' leadership.[41] Ten of the twelve spies sent to explore Canaan "spread among the Israelites a bad report," causing that entire generation of people to rebel and miss their opportunity to enter Canaan.[42] Most of the prophetic literature from Jeremiah to Malachi is devoted to systemic societal sin. Jesus rebuked groups of people, from entire regions to large bodies of religious leaders.[43] The Apostle Paul spoke of the spiritual blindness of a nation.[44] John's letter revealed God's frustration with entire church communities.[45] What makes community sin so dangerously deceptive is that certain ways of thinking and acting become normalized within a social structure.

---

[38] Gen. 18:16—19:29.

[39] Gen. 37.

[40] Ex. 1.

[41] Num. 1–50.

[42] Num. 13–14.

[43] Matt. 11:21; 23:13–29.

[44] Rom. 11:25–26.

[45] Rev. 2—3.

In its extreme form, social sin gives rise to things like slave trades, racist policies, internment camps and mass genocides. Examples abound in company cultures, government policies, entertainment industries, political parties and even religious organizations. Groups of people can and do get it wrong, and the power of group dynamics makes it easier for them to defend their actions. Sometimes we are sinned against by others, whether individuals or groups of people who have united in their adoption of harmful ideas and practices. That is why the Proverbs teach us that we need to be careful and wise as we live our lives in this fallen world.[46] We cannot presume to know what is in the hearts of others, but we are right to be cautious.

There are times when our sin does, in fact, bring harm to us. This is one of the causes of our frustrations, and we must not sweep this aside. Suffering can be a direct consequence of our sin, whether our failure is intentional or unintentional. The biblical writers distinguish between "missing the mark" while trying to hit it (unintentional sin) and intentionally disobeying God (missing the mark while aiming in the other direction)—although both are considered a sin.[47] Even

---

[46] Prov. 14:15; 23:1–8.

[47] The Bible teaches that "missing the mark" (the most common Hebrew word for sin) is sin, but not all sin is treated the same in Scripture. This is one of the reasons why different types of sacrifices were offered as remedies for different types of sins. For example, ignorance is a form of sin, but it is not the same as rebellion. For an introductory discussion in a standard theological textbook, see Millard J. Erickson,

the most celebrated figures in Scripture have endured unspeakable pain because of their sin—from Abraham to Moses to David to Peter. Our sin can cause suffering. This is why we should be quick to take responsibility for ways we have failed and confess our sins to God daily.

Still, some explanations fall under the general category of the Fall, also referred to as Adam's curse or the curse of sin. Disease, difficulty, decay and ultimately death are all part of this world, and all of us feel this frustration almost every single day. We are broken, but so is our world. The whole of creation is groaning, longing for redemption.[48] We are longing for a new earth, the day when there will be no more death, crying or pain. Sometimes pandemics sweep through this world simply because it is fallen. As hard as we may try, we simply cannot prevent every disease, and although we should pursue effective cures, they only delay the inevitable. And so we long for the day when Christ returns and makes all things new. This is why we pray, "Come, Lord Jesus," and put an end to our suffering.[49] Come, and make all things new!

There are multiple explanations for pain and suffering and loss. Satan causes his fair share of chaos, and so do others. We contribute to the painful realities that come into our own lives. The fall, the curse of sin, also makes life difficult for all of us. It eventually takes

---

Christian Theology (Grand Rapids, MI: Baker Book House, 1985), 561–80.

[48] Rom. 8:22–24.

[49] Rev. 22:20.

away our very lives on this earth. All of these are part of the causes of pain and suffering.

The House of the Interpreter

In John Bunyan's classic work, *Pilgrim's Progress*, Christian is on a journey bound for Mount Zion. But he is not on this journey alone. Evangelist shares the good news. Help lifts him out of the Slough of Despond. Discretion guides him on the way. Hopeful never gives up on him. Faithful stays with him to the very end. And Goodwill takes him to the House of the Interpreter.[50] On this journey, we need community. We need all kinds of people, including spiritual guides, those like Bunyan's Interpreter, who understand Scripture and know how to apply it to the human soul. We are unwise to try to sort through all of the questions we have alone. I know this from experience! Kings need counselors, athletes (even the best in the world) need coaches, business leaders need expert advice, and followers of Jesus need guides.

If you are like me and want explanations amid some painful loss, it is often helpful to engage a trusted guide. In Anglican, Orthodox and Roman Catholic spirituality, these persons are often called spiritual directors. This is someone with good theological bones. It can be a godly mentor, a wise pastor, a spiritual director or a trusted counselor; someone to whom you can tell everything and know you can fully trust them. I prefer talking to someone with extensive training in

---

[50] John Bunyan, *The Pilgrim's Progress: from this World to That which is to Come*, eds. James Blanton Wharey and Roger Sharrock (Oxford, UK: Oxford University Press, 1967).

theology and soul care, as well as a person who is bound by sacred vows. I have learned the hard way that people can be loose with their lips. It is not safe to share your struggles with just anyone. The world is also a complicated place. Like Christian, we need an interpreter to help us see what we cannot see on our own.

What is the cause of the painful experience you are going through right now? Did Satan cause this? Was it someone else, someone driven by fear or jealousy or selfish ambition or spite—or maybe just plain ignorance? How have you contributed to the frustrations you are facing? Or perhaps the loss you have endured is just the result of living in a fallen world. I've discovered that it may not be a multiple-choice question at all. Unfortunately, it usually isn't. It could be more like a chemistry algorithm, when one particle interacts with another, setting off a chain reaction. And even the search itself can be difficult. It is almost never possible to speak of a person's motive (singular) because the heart is much more complicated. As Augustine said: "Man is himself a great mystery. The hairs of his head are numbered (Matt. 10.30) to you, and none of them is lost in you; but his hairs are more easily numbered than his feelings and the emotions of his heart."[51] So don't expect easy answers even when you go to the House of the Interpreter. And don't search for answers alone. One of my colleagues frequently quotes a line from the

---

[51] Augustine, *The Confessions* ed. Philip Burton, (New York, NY: Random House, 2001), 79. The precise quote can be found at 4.14.22 in most editions.

award-winning American writer Augusten Burroughs that I have found helpful. Recalling the good advice given to him by a friend during his battle with alcohol, he wrote: "Think of your head as an unsafe neighborhood; don't go there alone." [52] That's good advice. John Bunyan would have agreed.

In my own experience, I have come to expect only approximate answers when evaluating explanations for personal suffering and loss. I know that somewhere behind it all, Satan lurks. He is the Prime Mover and the cause of every catastrophe. He kills, steals and destroys. [53] We must pray for protection from the prowling lion that seeks to bring us harm. I also know that people are image-bearers capable of doing amazing things. Not everyone gets up in the morning thinking about ways to hurt us. That is a very distorted way of looking at people that will, in the end, prove harmful to us. Cynics, I've noticed, never talk about all the times they get it wrong. But image-bearers are flawed—they fear, they falter, they fail. They say and do some very painful things, and they may even cleverly hide their own motives. We must remember that we cannot prevent this. We must be neither cynical nor naïve. We must be as wise as we can with the recognition that we cannot prevent every sinful act of humanity from touching us. And then we must remember that we are

---

[52] Augusten Burroughs, *Dry: A Memoir* (New York, NY: St. Martin's Press, 2013), 157.

[53] John 10:10.

not "in the place of God."[54] He is the Judge, and he will do what is right.

We also make our fair share of contributions to our own misery. We fall short of God's law and the expectations we have for ourselves. Our thoughts and deeds bring pain and suffering and loss. We must take time to examine our own hearts, perhaps even with someone to help us, if necessary. We must confess and seek forgiveness for our sin daily—and even ask God to cleanse us from those sins of the heart that he has not yet revealed to us.

I also know that the curse of sin hangs over this world like a pall. Loss is part of this world for the holiest of saints, and death is a constant reminder. Together, we long for the coming of the Kingdom of God. What we must avoid at all costs are our kneejerk attempts to cobble together simple answers in times of loss. In fact, sometimes, the best we can do in the face of mysterious loss is to express our pain to God and pray for his grace. In his recent work *God and the Pandemic: A Christian Reflection On The Coronavirus And Its Aftermath*, N. T. Wright offers sage counsel for our own day:

> In a time of crises, when death sneaks into houses and shops, when you may feel healthy yourself but you may be carrying the virus without knowing it, when every stranger on the street is a threat, when we go around wearing masks, when churches are shut and people are dying with nobody to pray by

---

[54] Gen. 50:20.

their bedside—this is a time for lament. For admitting that we don't have easy answers.[55]

It is not wrong to search for answers in this complicated world, but we must take time to grieve and pray. And given the complexity of life in this world, it is unwise to spend too much time trying to provide tidy answers. Life is just going to be a little messy until Christ returns and reveals everything, even the secrets of every person's heart.[56] Contemplative introspection can very quickly turn into unhelpful naval gazing. Before long, we are no longer reflecting on the past with the goal of moving forward more wisely. Instead, we are stuck in the past, completely unable to make the kind of progress we desire. Sometimes we must simply accept that God, in his sovereign wisdom and goodness, perhaps through a rather complicated plot in our story, has brought some privation into our lives. We need healing more than we need explanations. Flourishing in the future is better than figuring out the past.

We are just told: "Now there was a famine in the land, besides the famine that was in the days of Abraham." And then we are told that Isaac listened to the voice of God.

---

[55] N. T. Wright, God and the Pandemic: A Christian Reflection on the Coronavirus and Its Aftermath (Grand Rapids, MI: Zondervan, 2020), 53–4.

[56] 1 Cor. 4:5.

2

The Blessing

The LORD appeared to Isaac and said, "Do not go down to Egypt; live in the land where I tell you to live. Stay in this land for a while, and I will be with you and will bless you. For to you and your descendants I will give all these lands and will confirm the oath I swore to your father Abraham. I will make your descendants as numerous as the stars in the sky and will give them all these lands, and through your offspring all nations on earth will be blessed, because Abraham obeyed me and did everything I required of him, keeping my commands, my decrees and my instructions." So Isaac stayed in Gerar.
— Genesis 26:2–5

In the days of Abraham, Isaac and Jacob, people often moved to Egypt during famines. In the land of the great pharaohs, the Nile River nourished a large swath of land that stretched some four thousand miles from the heart of Africa to the Mediterranean. Abraham went to Egypt during the famine in his day. Isaac's son, Jacob, would also go to Egypt and bring his entire family with him. Joseph, we learn later in Genesis, had actually been sent ahead by God to save many lives.

Recall what Joseph said to his brothers: "God sent me ahead of you to preserve for you a remnant on the earth to save your lives by a great deliverance."[57] The hatred of Joseph's brothers and their bitter betrayal was somehow part of God's plan to save the family. God was sending Joseph ahead to get things ready. This is mysterious providence indeed!

Egypt would have been the most natural place for Isaac to take his family. It was a big move, a journey of several weeks or more along the Via Maris, the ancient coastal highway between Canaan and Egypt. In Egypt, there were cities and towns teeming with people living near the longest river in the world. There would be pasture for Isaac's cattle and marketplaces for buying and selling. There was the port city of Canopus (near modern-day Alexandria), where international trade flourished. A quaint farming community in the rich soils of the Nile Delta was also a promising location. And there was Giza, a bustling city with a skyline of pyramids and ample opportunity for a clever man like Isaac. Egypt was the place to be in famine.

During the unexplained famine, Isaac moved from the Negev, the desert regions of Palestine (near modern-day Beersheba), to the city of Gerar, closer to the Mediterranean coast. The approximate area around Gerar is in the vicinity of today's Eshkol National Park, a place of desert palms and fecund fields. Isaac's personal relationship with the king of Gerar and his access to the palace implies that the patriarch had

---

[57] Gen. 45:7.

already become a person of significant regional influence. The patriarchs were not lonely nomads roaming the desert. Isaac, like his father, was more akin to a desert prince with a retinue of servants to manage his affairs. His need to relocate during the famine was due in part to the vast operation he had inherited from his father. A move to the coast was likely a temporary measure allowing him to take care of his family, protect his flocks and wait out the famine before returning to Beersheba. His friendship with a king, another sign of his influence, would give him access to people of power and open doors for trade. So "Isaac went to Abimelech, king of the Philistines."[58]

He may have already decided that a move to Egypt was inevitable when the Lord appeared to him in some unmistakable fashion. These kinds of apparitions were rare, but they did happen. Many of the visions recorded in Scripture were like lucid dreams, causing the heart to palpitate with fear, leaving the dreamer startled, even frightened, and unable to return to sleep. The Lord spoke to him and said, "Do not go down to Egypt; dwell in the land of which I will tell you. Sojourn in this land, and I will be with you and bless you."[59] It was clear. God did not want Isaac to go to Egypt. So, he stayed in Canaan, near the Philistine city of Gerar.

---

[58] Gen. 26:1.

[59] Gen. 26:2–3.

Hearing God's Voice

It is not always easy to know what to do when we are going through hard times. Solutions aren't always simple, and that is why we are told to pray for wisdom when we are going through all kinds of trials.[60] The call to pray for wisdom implies that God wants his people to think, to reflect, to mull things over and to consider the wisest course of action. He promises to give us the wisdom we need in such times when we ask in faith. There are many things to take into consideration during times of famine. Isaac was contemplating a big move; he had a lot to think about. There are some Christians who want to simply suspend all judgment and ask God to tell them what to do during difficult times. But God has endowed us with the faculty of reason, and he never commends an empty head as a great virtue. On the contrary, he tells us to search for wisdom and knowledge like we are on a quest for buried treasure. He reminds us that the ability to navigate through this perilous life is a gift from God that could save our very lives.[61] The Scriptures are clear on this. Isaac's move to Gerar seemed to be a good course of action, and considering a move to Egypt was also wise.

But there are times when God seems to show up in the most unexpected ways and tell us to do something. This is clearly what happened to Isaac while he was pondering a move to the Nile Valley. There are some

---

[60] James 1:2–5.

[61] Proverbs 2–4 are poems in praise of knowledge and wisdom intended to encourage the people of God to seek after these valued treasures of God.

Christians who want to deny that God actually speaks to us today. I will admit that I did lean in this direction early in my own theological journey. But I have now come to believe that we must be seekers of wisdom and open to the wonder of God's mysterious guidance during our sojourn on this earth. I think this change came about through my encounter with Christians in the non-Western world, who read passages about dreams and visions differently than I did. They look at me strangely when I tell them about nineteenth-century hermeneutical developments in America that require them to read the Bible differently! We must pray and think and use our heads. We should listen to counsel, get all the facts and weigh all the odds. However, I have come to believe that we should also be open to God doing something that just wows us—that makes it clear that He wants us to do something unusual. God wanted Isaac to stay in Canaan, even though Egypt would have been a very good place to go. I will talk more about what I call the "way of wisdom and wonder" in the final chapter and offer a little more guidance on decision-making amid difficult times.

Sojourners

God makes it clear to Isaac that he is not to go to Egypt, even though it seemed like a good move. Instead, he is told to "sojourn" in Canaan, a Hebrew word that means to live somewhere as a foreigner, as someone who has fewer rights than a permanent resident. [62]

[62] Brown, Driver and Briggs, *Hebrew and English Lexicon*, 157.

Along with this command to stay in a place that seemed so unpromising was God's promise to be with him and bless him. Here is an important word of encouragement for all who follow in the footsteps of Abraham, Isaac and Jacob. God promises to be with us wherever we go. And with his presence, there is blessing.

The presence and blessing of God are not somehow confined to one geographic location. Yahweh is not a local deity to be found only on the Nile River. He is with his people, and he can bless them even in the desert. God can and does bless his followers in some of the most unexpected places. He is our Shepherd, he provides all our needs, he refreshes our souls, and he is even with us through the darkest valley.[63] He says to his children, "Never will I leave you; never will I forsake you."[64] This promise is for us! As followers of Jesus, we are sojourning in this land. We are waiting, longing for the kingdom to come, for the day when he makes all things new. We are living in hope for that day when he will wipe away every tear from our eyes. He has promised, "I am making everything new!" He has reassured us, "Write this down, for these words are trustworthy and true."[65] But we can still flourish where we are.

While we are on our way to our true home in the City of God, he is with us right now. He promises to bless and keep us even during our sojourn in this life.

---

[63] Ps. 23.

[64] Heb. 13:5.

[65] Rev. 21:4–6.

The priestly blessing was given to the people of God while they were in the wilderness![66] He provides many joys along the way, good things to eat and drink, time with family and friends, grace that is sufficient for every trial, and he tells us to enjoy our life as much as we possibly can in this season of sojourn.[67] Still, we are sojourners. In his classic work *The Problem of Pain*, C. S. Lewis observed that "settled happiness and security" eludes us in this world, though God has still "scattered broadcast" significant "joy, pleasure and merriment." As he captured it so vividly in one of my favorite Lewis tropes: "Our Father refreshes us on the journey with some pleasant inns, but will not encourage us to mistake them for home."[68] We are sojourners, just like Isaac. And God can bless us in the land of our sojourning even while we look forward to the greatest blessings in our true home.

Are These Promises for Us?

All this talk of blessing may leave some readers wondering if these kinds of promises are really for us. Our friends in Africa and much of the non-Western world read the Bible differently than many Western people who have been shaped by modern interpretive

---

[66] Num. 6:23–27.

[67] Ecc. 9:9.

[68] C. S. Lewis, *The Problem of Pain* (New York, NY: HarperCollins, 2001), 116.

developments since the Enlightenment. [69] My engagement with theological reflection in Africa has encouraged me to find greater solidarity with my biblical ancestors. Many American readers have been exposed to theological developments in the West that need sorting out. A potted work like this is hardly the place for solving these problems, though I do want to provide what I hope will be some helpful guidance on this particular theme of human flourishing.

God was very specific when he said he would "bless" Isaac and give "these lands" to him and his "offspring." He was emphasizing again the promise he had given to his father, Abraham. As already observed, the commentators have argued that this text serves as a bridge between Abraham and Jacob, showing God's faithfulness to continue to bless his people from one generation to the next. What about these promises to Isaac for things like land and children and influence? Furthermore, what do we do with what appears to be an exception clause? Is the blessing of God contingent on "obeying" God's "voice" and keeping his "commandments"? Theologians have spilled a lot of ink over these questions. I would like to offer a few comments and do so without derision toward those who may disagree. The latter question, the relationship between obedience and blessing, I will discuss at greater

---

[69] For an introduction to the way many non-Western people look at Scripture, see Philip Jenkins, *The New Faces of Christianity: Believing the Bible in the Global South* (Oxford, UK: Oxford University Press, 2006).

length in the next chapter when we look at Isaac's deception.

There are some theologians who read passages filled with promises of material blessings and limit the application to the people of Israel. They want to say something like, "The physical blessings were for Israel, but the spiritual blessings are for us!" Traces of this line of interpretation can be found in the writings of the African exegete Origen of Alexandria (185–253), though, to be fair, his eccentric approach to biblical interpretation allowed for multiple layers of meanings. In the nineteenth century, influential British and American thinkers developed a system of biblical interpretation known as dispensationalism. This interpretive grid divides the promises of God into "dispensations" (or periods of time), with the Old Testament promises about land and children and flourishing applying to Israel. The Church, that is, modern-day Christians, inherit the "spiritual" blessings of salvation through Israel. This is a simplistic explanation of a rather technical interpretive system, but it is a helpful summary. This way of reading Scripture was popularized during the twentieth century by one of the best-selling study Bibles of all time, *The Scofield Reference Bible*.[70] This way of reading the Bible is also one of the reasons many evangelical Christians believe that the modern-day nation of Israel has an undisputed right to the land of Israel. The promises to

---

[70] Todd R. Mangum and Mark S. Sweetnam, *The Scofield Reference Bible: Its History and Impact on the Evangelical Church* (Colorado Springs, CO: Paternoster, 2009).

ancient Israel are literal and eternal, and political will and military power are sometimes used to fulfill them! But they are not for modern-day Christians who are not Jews. In essence, the promises to Israel and the promises to the non-Jewish Church have been distinguished. And if they are not, then modern-day Christians should also be claiming land rights in Jerusalem![71] While I grew up imbibing this sort of theology from my fundamentalist pastor, I have come to find this system to be incoherent and confusing in many places. I now side with the majority of biblical interpreters who see this approach to interpretation as novel and narrow.[72] I will include more below on what I think is a better way.

There is also a ditch on the other side of the road that we must avoid. There are those who preach what has become known as the prosperity gospel, that if we just have enough faith, we can have our best lives now. This teaching takes the biblical passages on blessing and flourishing seriously, but it tends to downplay or ignore other important issues, like sin and suffering. It is a quintessential American theology that has now, unfortunately, been exported to many parts of the

---

[71] For a history of the political implications of this interpretive approach, as well as a more nuanced defense of Christian Zionism on other grounds, see Gerald R. McDermott, *The New Christian Zionism: Fresh Perspectives on Israel and the Land* (Downers Grove, IL: IVP Academic, 2016).

[72] The literature on this is extensive. For the most fair-minded critique written in readable prose by an established theologian, see Vern S. Poythress, *Understanding Dispensationalists* (Phillipsburg, NJ: P&R Publishing, 1986).

developing world.[73] There are at least two major flaws in prosperity theology. The first problem is that it glosses over so much of the suffering and setbacks found in the biblical narrative, even in the lives of those people who were truly blessed! Job is the classic example. The second problem is that while it does emphasize physical blessings in the here and now (something that I think is good), it tends to place most of the emphasis on the present. The stress is laid on God creating all things for our enjoyment, but what is missing is the clear biblical teaching that if all our hope is in this life, we are of all people most miserable.[74] It takes the present seriously, it emphasizes the promises of God for this life, but it places too much hope in the present. The resurrection is the best part of the good news. No amount of faith can conjure up utopian life on this earth.

So, what is the answer? It is better, in my view, to see greater continuity between the testaments, and therefore greater applicability of the Scriptures for all people at all times.[75] The Church is the New Israel, and the promises of God to bless his people are for all his people. He is concerned about our lives now—and our lives in the long tomorrow. The godly life has "value for all things, holding promise for both *the present life* and the

---

[73] Kate Bowler, *Blessed: A History of the American Prosperity Gospel* (New York, NY: Oxford University Press, 2013).

[74] I Cor. 15:19.

[75] The most helpful scholarly discussion of this theme can be found in John S. Feinberg, ed., *Continuity and Discontinuity: Perspectives on the Relationships Between the Old and New Testaments* (Westchester, IL: Crossway Books, 1988).

life to come [italics mine]."[76] God is concerned about
our bodies and souls. We should pray that our friends
"may enjoy good health and that all may go well" with
them just as we pray for their spiritual prosperity![77] He
is concerned about our everyday lives here on this earth.
We are "valued" by our Father in heaven who cares
about what we eat and drink and the clothing we
wear.[78] And as C. S. Lewis quipped, "There's no good
trying to be more spiritual than God. God never meant
man to be a purely spiritual creature." [79] The Old
Testament helps us keep our feet firmly planted on the
earth, even as the New Testament encourages us to look
forward to the kingdom of God while we are here. And
yes, land will be part of the deal. While politicians try to
sort out where the American Embassy should be located
in Israel, this really has very little to do with our future
hope. We are enjoying material and spiritual blessings
now, even while we wait for the new heavens and the
new earth—and the New Jerusalem.

Therefore, I think it is best to read the promises of
God to bless Abraham and Isaac and their descendants
with material and spiritual blessings as true for every
generation. This is clearly how Israel and the early
Christians (most of whom were Jews!) understood these
passages. It is also one of the primary reasons these

---

[76] I Tim. 4:8.

[77] 3 John 2.

[78] Matt. 6:25–33.

[79] C. S. Lewis, *Mere Christianity* (New York: NY:
HarperCollins, 2001), 64.

promises were written down—to encourage every
subsequent generation to place their hope in a God who
wants to bless us and keep us now and forever. The
coming of Christ did not cancel God's promise to bless
his people with material blessings, replacing all the
earthy blessings with spiritual ones. The gospel enlarges
rather than limits our understanding of blessing. Our
God shall supply all our needs, even granting us many
of the desires of our hearts. But we cannot live on bread
alone; he has given us his word, and the greatest
blessing of all—Christ forever. We can have a good life
now, but the best life is yet to come!

It is also good to temper our expectations by trusting
in a God who sovereignly bestows his blessings upon his
children—whether Abraham, or Isaac, or Jacob or
Joseph or you or me. When the Psalmist wrote: "The
boundary lines have fallen to me in pleasant places," he
was at once praising God for the gift of God while
confessing that he is the one who draws up our
boundary lines.[80] If I may say it this way: God blesses
us, but he decides how much property we should own
and where the "boundary lines" fall. I think we may say
that God chooses to bless his people in all kinds of ways,
providing all kinds of "pleasant inns" on the journey,
though his greatest blessings await us in our true home.

Yes, this doctrine is open to abuse, but this does not
make it wrong. The so-called prosperity gospel has
distorted the truth, but their abuse of a good doctrine
does not make the doctrine untrue. The sermon to the

[80] Ps. 16:5–6.

Hebrews is, in my view, overlooked as a great help to the Church on this question. Noah, Abraham, Isaac, Jacob, David, Solomon, Samson and the prophets are held up as examples to the followers of Jesus. They lived by faith, and they were blessed during their lives on this earth with material *and* spiritual blessings.[81] But they all awaited the future promises of even greater blessing. We can read the promises of God to bless our forefathers and believe that he is a God who blesses his people in every generation. We have placed our faith in a good God, who satisfies us with many good things in this life, even as we place our hope in the greatest blessing of all—Jesus Christ and the great future that awaits us in the eternal kingdom of God.

So, when you read about God's desire to bless his people—take it seriously. Let the promises of God to bless you and encourage you to live with all your might in this life. We should not abide a reading of Scripture that wants somehow to limit the promises of God to the patriarchs, or assign them to a modern political state, or put a cap on them so that they can only be enjoyed in the future. The New Testament does not replace the Old Testament; instead, it recites it. We should not disparage the God-given blessings of children and land and bread and wine—the gospel teaches us to follow

---

[81] Paul speaks of the spiritual blessings given to Israel in Romans 3:1–8, using this to show that they are even more culpable (not less) than Gentiles. They were given "the very words of God" (Rom. 3:1). Israel was blessed with material and spiritual wealth.

Christ that we may "love life and see good days," even now.[82] It is our duty to obey and God's delight to bless.

[82] I Pet. 3:9, citing Ps. 34:12.

3

The Deceiver

So Isaac stayed in Gerar. When the men of that place asked him about his wife, he said, "She is my sister," because he was afraid to say, "She is my wife." He thought, "the men of this place might kill me on account of Rebekah, because she is beautiful." When Isaac had been there a long time, Abimelek king of the Philistines looked down from a window and saw Isaac caressing his wife Rebekah. So Abimelek summoned Isaac and said, "She is really your wife! Why did you say, 'She is my sister'?" Isaac answered him, "Because I thought I might lose my life on account of her." Then Abimelek said, "What is this you have done to us? One of the men might well have slept with your wife, and you would have brought guilt upon us." So Abimelek gave orders to all the people: "Anyone who touches this man or his wife shall surely be put to death."

—Genesis 26:2–5

The celebrated American Bible teacher James Montgomery Boice (1938–2000) titled his exposition of

Genesis 26: "The Sins of the Father."[83] For Boice, who is known for his faithful exposition of Scripture, this entire narrative is about how "Isaac exhibited the same lack of faith" as his father and "repeated the same sin."[84] He spends the lion's share of his exposition rehearsing Isaac's misdeeds, comparing them with our own modern bent toward fickleness and faithlessness. He first explains that "Isaac's First Failure" was in going to Gerar in unbelief, though this is nowhere even inferred in the biblical narrative as a sinful choice. His journey to Gerar was simply a pragmatic relocation to provide for his family during a famine. In fact, Isaac is actually commanded by God to remain in the vicinity of Gerar, and God blesses him abundantly! "Isaac's Second Sin," as Boice rightly shows, is lying about his marriage. This deception, as we will see, is far worse than a cursory reading of the text would suggest.

While Boice's exposition contains appropriate biblical warnings about the dangers of disobeying God, it largely misreads the narrative. God protected and blessed Isaac, despite his folly, just as he protected and blessed Abraham, despite his foolishness! And he protects Isaac in the most unlikely way—through a pronouncement by a Philistine king. The message of protection and blessing is so clear in the passage that even Boice, whose sermon largely misses the point (a rarity for such a great expositor), concedes in the end

[83] James Montgomery Boice, "The Sins of the Father," in *Genesis: An Expositional Commentary, Volume 2* (Grand Rapids, MI: Zondervan, 1985), 270–81.

[84] *Ibid.*, 271.

that God nowhere condemns Isaac or even his father for their sin. Instead, he blesses them! This should not lead us to think that the biblical writer is condoning sin. He is only showing the faithfulness of God to his people despite their failures. Here is a word of encouragement to every one of us. God doesn't bless perfect people. If that were his policy, no one would be blessed.

Abraham, Isaac and all their children down to the present day are people of faith who are capable of impressive acts of courage. Abraham left kith and kin in the place he had called home, obeying the voice of God in faith, "even though he did not know where he was going."[85] He simply "obeyed and went," believing that God would somehow provide for him and his family in a new land that he had never even seen. He later binds the hands and feet of his only son, Isaac, the son of promise, in order to offer him up as a sacrifice to God.[86] Isaac would have no doubt remembered this traumatic event in his own life. Abraham's faith in God would be considered sheer fanaticism by modern standards. This is faith that almost defies reason! But people of faith are also deeply flawed. The very same person who is so fulsomely praised in the Scriptures as the "the friend of God"[87] and the father of our faith, slept with his wife's maidservant because he did not trust that God would actually give him a son through his wife, Sarah.[88]

---

[85] Heb. 11:8–11.

[86] Heb. 11:17–18.

[87] James 2:23.

[88] Gen. 16:1–4.

Abraham (and Sarah), it seems, felt the need to help God deliver on his promises. When the father of our faith traveled to Egypt during a famine, he lied to Pharaoh about his wife, saying that she was his sister. He feared that a jealous official without moral scruples might imperil his own life. It was also a clever way of becoming friends with a powerful king and his court.[89] The ruse worked. The king "treated Abram well for her sake, and Abram acquired sheep and cattle, male and female donkeys, male and female servants, and camels."[90] He lied about his wife again when he was in Gerar, even allowing her to be taken into the household of a Canaanite king who had every intention of sleeping with her.[91] Isaac did the same thing. He lied and said he wasn't a married man—and that his beautiful wife was available to be courted! He likely followed in his father's footsteps because he saw there was some efficacy in the ploy (more on this below). We are no different. Father and son, and all who are the children of Abraham, are people of faith who are also deeply flawed.

A Bundle of Paradoxes

Faith is mixed with fear in this story. Isaac's fears, like his father's, appear to have been unfounded. As we know all too well, fear has a way of distorting reality, warping our perception and causing us to act in ways that are otherwise irrational. Isaac's sin, like his father's,

---

[89] Gen. 12:10–20.

[90] Gen. 12:16.

[91] Gen. 20:1–10.

does appear absurd. But that is because we are distant observers. We all know what it is like to fear. And anytime we live in fear, we too are capable of what is otherwise unthinkable. Isaac's deception, like his father's, was far worse than we might initially think. In the world that was inhabited by Abraham and Isaac, diplomatic marriages were a means of joining powerful families to acquire wealth and neutralize enemies.[92] This practice is widely attested in the world of the biblical patriarchs, as well as the kingdoms of David and Solomon.[93] Abraham and Isaac were men of influence and wealth, prince-like figures who were friends with powerful people wherever they moved. They had learned to survive and prosper in the cut and thrust of a dangerous world. A ruler might extend lavish hospitality and feign friendship only to uncover information he could use against you when the time presented itself.[94] Or he could become a powerful ally! The "wife-sister" deception was a way of keeping "friends close and

---

[92] The nature of diplomatic marriage in the ancient world also sheds light on the problems associated with Esau's marriage to Hittite wives, referenced at the end of the same chapter (26:34–35). Marriage did not just bring two people together; it brought entire families, ethnic groups and even nations together. This was no doubt a mixed blessing.

[93] For the background on this, see A. Malamat, "Aspects of the Foreign Policy of David and Solomon," *Journal of Near Eastern Studies*, Vol. 22, No. 1 (January 1963): 1–17; Alan R. Schulman, "Diplomatic Marriage in the Egyptian New Kingdom," *Journal of Near Eastern Studies*, Vol. 38, No. 3 (July 1979): 177–93.

[94] Prov. 23:1–3.

enemies closer," allowing Isaac, like his father, to buy time while making deals at the dinner table that would make him wealthy. He was currying favor with a king and using his beautiful wife to remain friends with court officials.[95] Everyone thought Isaac's wife was the most eligible virgin in the land, and marrying into the family of a wealthy sheik had significant promise! A close alliance with a powerful ruler gave Isaac access to opportunities and raised his prospects in the community.[96] Isaac had learned from his father to use his attractive wife to play kings and court officials. He was protecting himself while profiting from the deception. It was shrewd. It was wrong.

Isaac's duplicitous scheme was serendipitously exposed. The king happened to glimpse a flirtatious moment between Isaac and Rebekah while looking out the window of his palace. There is a play on words in the Hebrew text. Isaac's name means "to laugh" or "to sport"—in modern English, it can even mean to joke or play around. The same Hebrew root is used for what Isaac was doing with his wife—"laughing" (NIV), probably in a flirtatious or even sensual way. It was clear to the king that they were not brother and sister— they were actually lovers. Hebrew listeners would have been entertained by the clever pun. Isaac, the man whose name means to "fool around" is caught "fooling

---

[95] Eugene F. Roop, *Genesis: Believer's Bible Commentary* (Scottdale, PA: Herald Press, 1977), 176.

[96] Victor H. Matthews, "The Wells of Gerar," *The Biblical Archaeologist*, Vol. 49, No. 2 (June 1986): 118–26.

around" with his own wife.[97] This deception had gone on for some time. As the text notes, this happened "when he had been there a long time." Abimelech confronts Isaac like an angry Old Testament prophet and then issues a royal order that no one should touch him or Rebekah. The effect of this detail is to show the irony of a Canaanite king rebuking a follower of God for his sin. Abimelech is portrayed as a person of steadfast morality, in contrast to Isaac's manipulative manner. More importantly, the turn of events is intended to reveal that God is watching over Isaac, even in the most unlikely way, by using a pagan king to protect him from his own folly.

This passage puts on display the paradox of the human condition. Isaac obeys God by staying in Gerar during a time of famine. Rather than going to Egypt, he goes against his instincts, trusting that God will take care of him and his family. At the same time, he is a person who battles hidden fears. He trusts God enough to stay in Gerar but feels the need to rely on deception in order to prosper in the land. Martin Luther (1483–1546) explained this reality five hundred years ago by saying that "The saints in being righteous are at the same time sinners." [98] Theologians captured this paradox in a Latin expression that has been translated

---

[97] Derek Kidner, *Genesis: An Introduction and Commentary* (Leicester, UK: Inter-Varsity Press, 1967), 153.

[98] Martin Luther, *Lectures on Romans*, ed. William Pauck (Louisville, KY: John Knox Press, 1961), 208.

into English as: "Simultaneously justified and sinners."[99] We are, Luther was saying, made righteous by God through faith in Christ, while we remain sinners who constantly fall short of the glory of God.

For Luther, this was a precious doctrine, for how else could a sinner find acceptance by God except through the free gift of justification by faith? We are so soiled by sin that we could never be good enough to enter the kingdom of God! The lives of the patriarchs illustrate this for us. Like Abraham and Isaac, we are people of faith, and yet we are still sinners. While we do trust God, we frequently do the things we don't want to do and don't do the things we want to do. We become overwhelmed with fear. We fail to trust God. As Brennan Manning put it so well:

> When I get honest, I admit I am a bundle of paradoxes. I believe and I doubt, I hope and I get discouraged, I love and I hate, I feel bad about feeling good, I feel guilty about not feeling guilty. I am trusting and suspicious. I am honest and I still play games. Aristotle said I am a rational animal; I say I am an angel with an incredible capacity for beer.[100]

We are all like Abraham and Isaac. We are created in the image of God, capable of courageous faith, and

---

[99] Alister E. McGrath, *IUSTITIA DEI: A History of the Doctrine of Justification* (Cambridge, UK: Cambridge University Press, 1998), 209.

[100] Brennan Manning, *The Ragamuffin Gospel* (Colorado Springs, CO: Multnomah Books, 2005), 11.

yet we are sinners who disappoint God, others and ourselves. We are a "bundle of paradoxes." And the good news is that somehow God still blesses us.

The Godward Life

This story, and the patriarchal narratives in general, raise the question of how we should understand the relationship between obedience and blessing. It is hard to deny that there is some relationship between the two, even in this text. [101] Returning again to our earlier reading, we recall that God appeared to Isaac in a vision and told him that he had blessed his father because he "obeyed me in everything I required of him, keeping my commands, my decrees and my instructions." [102] The clear implication of these words was to tell Isaac that if he followed in his father's footsteps by obeying God, he, too, would be blessed. But what exactly does this mean? The law had not yet been given, so the reference to "commands" and "decrees" and "instructions" cannot refer to the Law of Moses, at least not in the case of Abraham, Isaac and Jacob. Further, as we have already observed, Abraham's life was far from perfect! So the phrase, "Abraham obeyed me and did everything I required of him," cannot be interpreted in absolutist fashion. The most reasonable explanation is that the writer of Genesis is encouraging later followers of God to emulate the faithful *direction* of Abraham's life. Father and son

---

[101] Kidner, *Genesis*, 153.

[102] Gen. 26:5.

were far from perfect. But they were completely devoted to the Lord. They were living what some theologians have called "the Godward life," something that speaks of the entire orientation of one's life. Their entire lives moved in the direction of the Divine. Yes, they stumbled along the way, but they were moving in the right direction. Thus the Hebrew words translated "commands" and "decrees" and "instructions" are what commentators refer to as "heaped-up terms," suggesting that Abraham was entirely devoted to God.[103] And this is the life that God blesses.

Therefore, it is best to interpret these words as God's way of providing a summary statement on Abraham's life, leaving out the parenthetical comments and critical footnotes that dwell on his failures and foibles. His sins are recorded to warn us, but this is not how God summarizes Abraham's life. It is kind of like telling someone about a son or daughter who has made you proud. What do we often do? We brag on them, describing their best qualities with effusive praise. God is telling Isaac about Abraham, describing the devotion of his heart and the direction of his life. Abraham was a remarkable man of faith, but he was still a sinner. And what did Isaac do after receiving this vision from God? "He stayed in Gerar." Like father, like son, Isaac heard the voice of God and obeyed him. Father and son both failed miserably, but they were completely devoted to God and determined that the direction of their lives would be *Godward*. When God's people who had been given the Torah heard these stories, they were also

---

[103] Kidner, *Genesis*, 153.

encouraged to be devoted to God and obey His commands, decrees and laws given by Moses.[104] They, like Abraham and Isaac, would also sin. That is why obedience to the commands, decrees and laws of the Torah included the offering sacrifices for their sins to God. The prophets were constantly encouraging them to follow closely after God so that they might be blessed.

A Word to Seekers

For those who are reading this book as seekers, I want to say a word here about salvation and its relationship to obedience. Followers of Jesus from long ago and far away, from whatever denominational background, do not believe that people are saved by obedience to God. Such a notion would leave our salvation in complete doubt. "There is no one righteous; not even one."[105] Instead, the Scriptures point in a different direction, teaching that salvation is by the grace and mercy of God because of Christ who died in our place and was raised to life to give us life. This does not mean that good works are unimportant. It only means that obedience is not the cause of our salvation. Faith in the death, burial and resurrection of Jesus is what makes a person right with God. This is at the very center of our Christian faith. There are debates within the Christian tradition about how this all works, but there is no doubt that it does! As C. S. Lewis put it, "The central Christian belief is that Christ's death has

---

[104] Waltke, *Genesis*, 368–9.

[105] Rom. 3:23.

somehow put us right with God and given us a fresh start."[106] We call this the gospel—an old English word that means "good news."

This does not mean good works are unimportant—or even optional! The Scriptures teach us that we should be people who are "doing good" and "loving our neighbor," caring for orphans and widows, visiting the sick and imprisoned, being kind to friends and enemies, forgiving those who have wronged us and working to make this world a better place. Good works are an important part of the Christian message, not as the cause of our salvation, but as the inseparable effect of our salvation. Abraham's obedience did not save him—nor was Isaac told he would be saved his good works. The Apostle Paul saw this clearly, holding up the patriarchs as an example of faith. As he put it, "Abraham 'believed God, and it was credited to him as righteousness.'"[107] Abraham's faith saved him, but his faith was expressed in his obedience to God. In this way, genuine faith changes the direction of a person's life. This is how we also make sense of the arguments laid out by James, the brother of Christ, who taught that works are inseparable (a word I used earlier) from faith. As he put it: "faith by itself, if it is not accompanied by action, is dead."[108] He was saying that genuine faith saves a person, and if that faith is real (alive rather than dead), it will be expressed in a person's actions. Is this

---

[106] Lewis, Mere Christianity, 54.

[107] Gal. 3:6.

[108] James 2:17.

not what we see in the lives of Abraham and Isaac? They respond to God in faith, and that faith was expressed in their obedience. Faith in God's gracious gift of Christ, who died for us, will change the direction of our lives and bless us forever.

Like Father, Like Son—Blessed!

This is the life that God blesses—the life that is moving in the right direction—the Godward life. This is the life that Isaac lived. The parallels between Isaac's story in Genesis 26 and his father's story in Genesis 20 are so remarkable that many commentators believe that there is some shaping of the patriarchal stories to intentionally link the narratives.[109] Even if it is allowed that there was some purposeful harmonizing (I would say, under the Spirit's guidance), it may be argued that the passages are intended to show that Isaac is the heir-apparent to the promises made by God to Abraham. In both narratives, there is a famine, a wife-sister tale, a king named Abimelech (a common name, and probably a predecessor), the promise of blessing and a resolution that ends in flourishing. As Old Testament scholar Gordon Wenham notes: "a conscious effort is being made to compare the career of Isaac with that of his father Abraham."[110]

This chapter does tell us about the "sins of the father," but it focuses more on the "blessings of the son." Isaac was a deeply flawed man, just like his father.

---

[109] Wenham, *Genesis 16–50*, 186.

[110] *Ibid.*, 187.

He lied to get ahead, just like his father before him. But he also enjoyed the undeserved favor of God upon his life. The sins of the father are handed down to the son, but so are the blessings of God. This interpretive direction flows with the current of the biblical narrative. The story is moving in the direction of blessing because of the sovereign goodness and faithfulness of God. The blessing of God is handed down from one generation to the next until the arrival of Christ. And then the blessing of God is passed down from one generation to the next, touching every one of us so that "the blessing given to Abraham might come" to us and be upon us forever![111]

If one re-reads the story in its entirety within the larger context of the Genesis narrative, the purpose of telling listeners about Isaac's deception becomes clearer. Isaac's indiscretion, rather than showing that the "sins of the father" are passed on to the son, is intended to demonstrate that the mercy and faithfulness of God are extended again and again to one generation after another. Abraham puts his wife, Sarah, in a precarious situation for his own gain on more than one occasion! And God directly intervenes. The way the Isaac story is written is also intended to show that Isaac's deception put husband and wife on a knife's edge. Rebekah could have been violated, but God intervened. As Wenham observes: "Once again the patriarch and his wife are saved from his folly by the mercy of God."[112] This story

---

[111] Gal. 3:14.

[112] Wenham, *Genesis 16–50*, 195

is not an encouragement to plunge headlong into sin while trusting that God will protect us from our folly. The Scriptures strongly warn us against such foolishness! Furthermore, there is almost always some kind of painful displeasure that comes from sinful choices. But the story does teach us not to despair when we have failed. We should follow the example of Abraham and Isaac by living a Godward life, one that is devoted to following him with all our might. But even when we are moving in the right direction, we will still fail. We will, like Abraham and Isaac, succumb to fear and do things in doubt. But if we persevere, if we are committed to "a long (and imperfect) obedience in the same direction," we can still look forward to blessing.[113] That is just how good and faithful God is.

---

[113] I have borrowed this phrase from Eugene H. Peterson, *A Long Obedience in the Same Direction: Discipleship in an Instant Society* (Downers Grove, IL: InterVarsity Press, 2019).

4

The Well Digger

Isaac planted crops in that land and the same year reaped a hundredfold, because the Lord blessed him. The man became rich, and his wealth continued to grow until he became very wealthy. He had so many flocks and herds and servants that the Philistines envied him. So all the wells that his father's servants had dug in the time of his father Abraham, the Philistines stopped up, filling them with earth. Then Abimelek said to Isaac, "Move away from us; you have become too powerful for us." So Isaac moved away from there and encamped in the Valley of Gerar, where he settled. Isaac reopened the wells that had been dug in the time of his father Abraham, which the Philistines had stopped up after Abraham died, and he gave them the same names his father had given them. Isaac's servants dug in the valley and discovered a well of fresh water there. But the herders of Gerar quarreled with those of Isaac and said, "The water is ours!" So he named the well Esek, because they disputed with him. Then they dug another well, but they quarreled over that one also; so he named it Sitnah. He moved on from there and dug another well, and no one quarreled over it. He named it Rehoboth, saying, "Now the Lord has given us room and we will flourish in the land."

    — Genesis 26:12–22

In the ancient world, well digging was hard work. It required skill, perspiration and perseverance. Only a few were masters of the trade, and this was one of the things that made wells so valued. Many of the ancient wells that have been uncovered by archaeologists beneath the sands of time were impressive achievements even by today's standards. They were usually more than just holes in the ground. It was not uncommon for skilled laborers to bore through several layers of rock, a project that might require several months of investment with no promise of finding water. Some wells looked more like a stairwell going down into a modern-day subway leading to a large underground spring—thus our modern English word "stairwell." There were also specially-designed wells, where fresh water would flow into an adjacent pool dressed with stone, similar to a fountain in a modern-day public park. Many wells were built around live springs, like the famous Gihon Spring in Jerusalem that dates back to the period of the patriarchs. My wife and I explored this impressive water source a few years ago in the old city of Jerusalem. Tourists are guided down a stairwell and through a vaulted tunnel nearly six hundred yards long that was carved under the City of David. The passage, known as the Siloam Tunnel or Hezekiah's Tunnel, follows the spring down to the Pool of Siloam in the Kidron Valley, a place that has provided fresh water to the people of

Jerusalem for more than 5,000 years.[114] Carving wells out of the land in Palestine was a remarkable achievement, and these water sources were essential for life in the ancient world.

Wells were places of flourishing. Cities, towns and villages prospered around springs, wells and pools. Flocks multiplied, herds increased, and crops grew. People opened markets and set up shop. Weary travelers came from afar to buy and sell, eat and drink. Friendships were formed, business deals were made, and the latest news was shared. People settled in places where water was plentiful; they built homes, had children, planted vineyards, and made a life for themselves. But fights could also break out in places of flourishing.

A successful well digger might draw unwelcome attention. In the land of Palestine, when an ambitious person struck water and opened up a place that made the desert bloom, others wanted in. A local ruler or a powerful sheik might stake a claim, arguing that the property actually belonged to him or his family or his deceased parents or a distant cousin. Land prices might go up. People would fight for control and jockey for position. Locals might come to loggerheads. And when

---

[114] Amihai Sneh, Ram Weinberger and Eyal Shalev, "The Why, How, and When of the Siloam Tunnel Re-evaluated," *The Bulletin of the American Schools of Oriental Research*, No. 359 (August 2010): 57–65; for a popular online article with illustrations, see "Hezekiah's Tunnel," *Biblical Archaeology Society*, August 13, 2013: https://www.biblicalarchaeology.org/scholars-study/tunnel/.

someone did flourish, it could breed sheer jealousy. Success, as we all know, has a way of attracting friends and enemies, as well as friends who may become future enemies. Cruel people may find a way to sabotage the hard work of a successful well digger. Someone may start a whisper campaign, driving a wedge between people, and causing a rift in relationships. That's what happened to Isaac.

The Well Digger

During his time in Gerar, Isaac prospered. God told him to stay in Palestine during the famine. Like his father, he obeyed, and he experienced the blessing of God. He inherited the wells his father Abraham had skillfully dug in the land of Gerar. Even after his wife-sister deception was exposed, he "planted crops in that land and the same year reaped a hundredfold, because the Lord blessed him."[115] He "became rich, and his wealth continued to grow until he became very wealthy."[116] Yes, Isaac worked hard, but the success he enjoyed was unmistakably due to the blessing of God. And then Isaac was told he was no longer welcome in Gerar. He had become too successful—too influential. "He had so many herds and servants that the Philistines envied him."[117] And then, "all the wells that his father's servants had dug in the time of his father Abraham, the

---

[115] Gen. 26:12.

[116] Gen. 26:13.

[117] Gen. 26:14.

Philistines stopped up, filling them with earth."[118] Even King Abimelech was worried about Isaac's growing influence. And so he told Isaac to leave: "Move away from us, you have become too powerful for us."[119] It's possible that Isaac's relationship with Abimelech had been strained by the wife-sister fiasco, but the primary reason the patriarch packed up his bags and moved was because of jealousy and fear.

Isaac could have stood his ground and protected the wells that had belonged to his father in Gerar. He could have insisted that this was the place God had told him to stay. The patriarchs, as we have already learned, were prince-like figures with significant regional power. They had armed servants, and they wielded influence. Abimelech knew this, and he wanted to neutralize Isaac's growing influence in Gerar. Abraham and his son Isaac had the ability to create regional coalitions large enough to bring down a king. Abraham had done this in Canaan (see Genesis 14), and Isaac was now more powerful than his father. The king was clearly afraid of the wealthy patriarch, and as we will see below, he would later pursue a peace accord with him.

But during this conflict in Gerar, Isaac chose not to put up a fight. We are not told why. It may be that Isaac wanted to avoid the risk. He may have been able to win, but at what cost to him and his family? Pyrrhic victories feel like defeats. It could be that Isaac was simply a man who loved peace. Personality likely played a role. We all

---

[118] Gen. 26:15.

[119] Gen. 26:16.

know people who get their hackles up in a hurry—who love to get into scrapes. Most people, I've discovered, find fighting to be an unpleasant affair. Isaac appears to be the kind of person who would just rather move on and find some other place to settle down with his family. This is how Shaul Bar describes Isaac in his study of the patriarch: "Isaac is portrayed as a peaceful person who did everything to keep the peace between his camp and his neighbors." [120] Whatever the motivation, Isaac's response required a certain degree of faith that God's blessing was not confined to the city of Gerar. He could flourish in a new place, as long as God was with him.

So, rather than fight in the place where he had enjoyed so much success, he moved away from the city into the Valley of Gerar. This area is now a national heritage site in Israel, known today as the Eshkol National Park. He would have still been near Gerar, but this move would provide some distance between him and Abimelech. And Isaac "reopened the wells that had been dug in the time of his father, which the Philistines had stopped up after Abraham died."[121] The reference to the wells being "stopped up after Abraham died" refers to an event that Isaac had likely witnessed as a younger man. It would have happened sometime after he had inherited his father's wealth, and likely a short time after his death. Isaac moved into the valley. He knew where to find the wells, but it would require significant excavation to reopen the water sources and

---

[120] Bar, *Isaac*, 2494.

[121] Gen. 26:17–18.

resettle his family and flocks. The fact that the water sources had remained closed shows that even the task of reopening old wells required significant skill and initiative. Isaac set to work, restored the old wells, and renamed them as a way declaring ownership and reclaiming what had previously belonged to his family.[122] He even "dug in the valley and discovered a well of fresh water there."[123] The Hebrew phrase for "well of fresh water" is literally, "living water," a reference to a remarkable discovery in the arid lands of Palestine—a fresh spring that is constantly flowing.[124] Isaac had been pushed out of the city, but he was now flourishing in the valley.

And then a fight breaks out. "The herdsmen of Gerar quarreled with Isaac's herdsmen and said, 'The water is ours!'"[125] It was a spurious claim. It was this valuable new discovery that set off the fight. As one commentator notes: "Isaac's wells are so valuable because they contain not just water, but *springing water*, that is, a spring that provides a constant supply of running water."[126] The patriarch had been blessed again, and this aroused jealousies again. Isaac's response demonstrates his frustration. He gives the well a one-word epitaph. It had been a source of blessing, but it became a source of contention. He renames it Esek, a

---

[122] Bar, *Isaac*, 2477.

[123] Gen. 26:19.

[124] Waltke, *Genesis*, 370.

[125] Gen. 26:20.

[126] Hamilton, *Genesis 18–50*, 202.

Hebrew word that means "to contend" or "to quarrel."[127] The oldest translation of the Hebrew, the Greek translation from the third century BC (known as the Septuagint), renders the word as "injustice." It's his way of cursing that place that had been a blessing.[128] *Esek!* Isaac's place of flourishing had caused a fight.

One question this text naturally raises is how we should respond when a fight breaks out and we feel like we have been wronged. It is not unusual for both sides to think they are right. That is usually what starts fights in the first place, and both sides become even more entrenched in the rightness of their cause. We should most certainly work to be peacemakers, and it is very possible that Isaac did his best to settle this dispute. Not only was it his disposition, he also had every incentive to settle matters in his new place of flourishing. He had already moved once. He had reopened his father's wells and discovered fresh springs in the valley. But peace eluded him.

Even our best efforts to make peace do not always yield the results we hope. We must do all we can to be at peace, but it is not always possible.[129] After we have done all that we can, there is always the option of standing our ground and finding other means of pursuing justice. Even then, there is a right way to go about the pursuit of justice. There are no easy answers

---

[127] Brown, Driver and Briggs, *Hebrew and English Lexicon*, 796.

[128] Wenham, *Genesis 16–50*, 192.

[129] Rom. 12:18.

when we fail to resolve the contention that comes into our lives. We are called to be peacemakers, but this word should not be construed to mean that we can somehow *make peace* happen by our own effort. Now that I am in the sixth decade of my pilgrimage on this earth, I have found peace is something we can and must work for, but in the end, it is only something God can give. Every situation has its own unique challenges, and one should always seek wise counsel before putting up a fight.[130]

There are times in this life when it is best simply to endure unjust treatment with faith in God. It takes a lot of self-discipline, but you need to know when to walk away from a fight and place all your faith in God. When we are on the wronged side, we are on the right side. Being wronged puts us in the position of power because God always sides with those who have been wronged. As King David was fleeing during a coup, a man named Shimei ran along the side of the road, cursing at him and throwing stones: "Get out, get out, your murderer, you scoundrel. The Lord has repaid you."[131] David, like Abraham, Isaac and Jacob before him, was a deeply flawed man. His failures are deeply disturbing my modern standards. When he was a young man, he was actually a William Wallace-like figure, plundering Philistine towns and leaving no witnesses alive while feigning fealty to local lords. His rise to power as king in Hebron, then in Jerusalem, was marked by intrigue and

---

[130] Prov. 20:18; 24:6.

[131] 2 Sam. 16:7–8.

bloodshed. His moral failure with Bathsheba and subsequent cover-up is a matter of public record. The deeds of his children, hidden behind palace walls, were scandalous. He may be one of the most complex figures in Scripture, "a man after God's own heart,"[132] a writer of poetry with deep affections for the divine, yet forbidden to build the Temple because of his violent reputation.[133] David is indeed a bundle of paradoxes! It is not surprising that some of his enemies were pleased to see the king run out of the city. As Shemei hurled stones and insults, the king's bodyguards reached for their swords and asked for leave to cut off his head. David said: "Leave him alone; let him curse, for the Lord has told him to. It may be that the Lord will look upon my misery and restore to me his covenant blessing instead of this curse today."[134] David accepted the curse as a blessing. He placed his faith in the Lord, who was looking upon his misery that very moment.

God is sovereign over the lips of sinful people, and he also hears the words they say. If we feel that a fight has broken out and we have been wronged, we must fix our eyes on the sovereignty of God. At times, it is best simply to move on in faith. That is what Isaac did. He moved on as peacefully as he could.

Archaeologists have made efforts to locate Isaac's wells, though we are not exactly sure where they are

---

[132] 1 Sam. 13:14.

[133] 1 Chron. 28:3.

[134] 2 Sam. 16:11–12,

today.[135] In the world Isaac inhabited, twenty miles was about a day's journey, and Isaac would have wanted to put more space between his family and his antagonists in Gerar—perhaps a trip requiring several days. So he packs up and moves. He looks for another location, relocates his family and digs another well, believing that God will bless him in a new place. He finds water again.

And another fight breaks out! "Then they dug another well; but they fought over that one also."[136] Another fight has broken out in a place of flourishing. So Isaac names the well Sitnah, which means adversary or opposition. The Hebrew word is literally "Adversary"—and from its root, we derive an English word that sounds very much like the Hebrew—Satan! Isaac literally names the well—"Satan" or "Adversary."[137] Isaac curses. *Sitnah!*

And then he gathers his family and his servants and his flocks and his herds, he packs up his belongings and moves again, further into the Palestinian desert in the middle of a famine. And the Well Digger digs again. And he finds water again. But this time, "no one quarreled over it," so he named it Rehoboth, which means "a broad, open place," or "room."[138] *Rehoboth!*, he says. *Finally, we have some room!* He gives praise to God: "The Lord has given us room, and we will flourish

---

[135] Wenham, *Genesis 16–50*, 192.

[136] Gen. 26:21.

[137] Brown, Driver and Briggs, *A Hebrew and English Lexicon*, 966.

[138] *Ibid.*, 932.

in the land."[139] Isaac continued to trust God, he kept on digging wells, and God gave him room to flourish in the desert in the middle of a famine.

Isaac's perseverance amid famine and frustration was an expression of his faith in God. He did not believe Egypt was the only place he could prosper. He did not limit God's grace to Gerar. God was with *him*. The blessing of God could not be contained in a river or confined to one hole in the ground. The Lord can bless his people anytime, anywhere! God had said to Abraham concerning Isaac's birth: "Is anything too hard for the Lord?"[140] Isaac's very existence was a miracle; surely, he could bless him in the desert! He could even turn "the desert into pools of water and the parched ground into a flowing spring."[141] When God's people recalled this narrative, after leaving Egypt and wandering through the desert, it gave them hope. In his recent biography on Isaac's life, Shaul Bar observes: "What we may perceive as weakness may have been his strength—he was patient and trusted God." Isaac never gave up. He kept the faith. He kept digging wells. He believed in the promise God made to bless him and his children. The story of this forgotten patriarch can encourage us to persevere, whatever difficulties or disappointments we may face. We can flourish in the desert. But we must keep the faith. And we must keep digging wells.

---

[139] Gen. 26:22.

[140] Ex. 18:14.

[141] Ps. 107:3.

Faith Works

Faith is not passive. Faith works. "By faith Noah built an ark to save his family."[142] "By faith Abraham made his home in the promised land like a stranger in a foreign country . . . as did Isaac and Jacob."[143] "By faith Abraham offered up Isaac as a sacrifice."[144] "By faith [Moses] left Egypt, not fearing the king's anger."[145] "By faith, the prostitute Rahab, because she welcomed the spies, was not killed."[146] "By faith" the people of God have "conquered kingdoms" and "administered justice" and "shut the mouth of lions" and "faced jeers and floggings."[147] People of faith are resilient! They never give up! Faith in the face of famine and frustration and foe pleases God, and those who come to him and earnestly seek him will be rewarded.[148] People of faith do mourn; they may even "curse" and lament in their prayers. But they do not give up. They persevere, not just because of God-endowed human strength, but because of their God-wrought faith in the unshakable promises of God to bless his people.

Origen of Alexandria (184–253) summarized this text: "He named the first well Injustice, the second he

---

142 Heb. 11:7.

143 Heb. 11:8–9.

144 Heb. 11:17.

145 Heb. 11:27.

146 Heb. 11:31.

147 Heb. 11:32–38.

148 Heb. 11:6.

named Enmity and the third he named Breadth; how true it is that God seems to allow all of these experiences into our lives—injustice, enmity and room."[149] We have all faced times of deprivation. We have probably all been asked to leave a place when we really wanted to stay. We have all experienced injustice because of a fight. We have all had enemies who delighted in our struggles. But we have also experienced the blessing of God, who gives us room to flourish! We must persevere in faith wherever God leads us. He is with us. He will bless us. As Origen captured it, "Let us never cease digging wells of living water."[150]

---

[149] Origen, *Homilies on Genesis and Exodus*, trans. Robert E. Heine (Washington, D.C.: The Catholic University Press of America, 1981), 186.

[150] *Ibid.*, 189.

5

The Peacemaker

From there he went up to Beersheba. That night
the Lord appeared to him and said, "I am the God
of your father Abraham. Do not be afraid, for I am
with you; I will bless you and increase the number
of your descendants for the sake of my servant
Abraham." Isaac built an altar there and called on
the name of the Lord. There he pitched his tent,
and there his servants dug a well. Meanwhile,
Abimelek had come to him from Gerar, with
Ahuzzath his personal advisor and Phicol the
commander of his forces. Isaac asked them, "Why
have you come to me, since you were hostile to me
and sent me away?" The answered, "We saw
clearly that the Lord was with you; so we said,
'There ought to be a sworn agreement between
us' — between us and you. Let us make a treaty
with you that you will do us no harm, just as we
did not harm you but always treated you well and
sent you away peacefully. And you are blessed by
God." Isaac then made a feast for them, and they
ate and drank. Early the next morning the men
swore an oath to each other. Then Isaac sent them
on their way, and they went away peacefully. That
day Isaac's servants came and told him about the
well they had dug. They said, "We've found

water!" He called it Shibah, and to this day the name of the town is Beersheba.

— Genesis 26:23–33

Beersheba is now the largest city in southern Israel. It is located in the Negev, the semi-arid region of southern Israel that roughly corresponds to the region from Hebron (near Jerusalem) down to the waterfront resort city of Eilat (Umm Al-Rashrash) on the northern tip of the Red Sea. The area is habitable, though it is dry. The word "Negev" is from a Hebrew root that means "dry" or "parched."[151] In 2005, Beersheba was designated as a World Heritage site by the United Nations Educational, Scientific and Cultural Organization (UNESCO) for its rich cultural history, much of it biblical in nature, dating back for thousands of years. Archaeological work at Beersheba has even unearthed one of the most sophisticated underground water-collection systems in the ancient world. [152] Beersheba became an urban city in the Negev during the days of Abraham, Isaac and Jacob, with "public structures, such as fortification walls, city gates, places and temples," providing indisputable evidence of a

[151] Brown, Driver and Brigs, *A Hebrew and English Lexicon*, 616.

[152] UNESCO, World Heritage List, "Biblical Tels— Megiddo, Hazor, Beer Sheba": https://whc.unesco.org/en/list/1108.

flourishing ancient community.[153] Beersheba has been a population center in the desert for thousands of years.

I took a camel ride in the Negev several years ago, and it reminded me of parts of Central and West Texas. I live in Austin, Texas, a place I fell in love with as a young boy, long before it became known as the Silicon Hills, home to tech companies like Amazon, AT&T, Dell, IBM, Nokia, PayPal, Roku, Tesla and Visa. The Texas Hill Country is a region in Central and West Texas with rugged hills of painted limestone festooned with colorful flowers, desert cacti, cedar scrub, scattered hardwoods and clear-water creeks. You can raise cattle and crops on this land if you have plenty of water. Beersheba looks like parts of this place I now call home—without the Colorado River. You have to dig to find water in Beersheba, but it's there. In 2015, Forbes Magazine even referred to the burgeoning city of Beersheba as the "a new silicon valley in the Middle East."[154] Beersheba, like Austin, is a good place to settle down and raise a family. It's a good place to live, and it was the place Isaac called home. But Austin, like

[153] Lily Singer-Avitz, "Household Activities at Tel Beersheba," in *Household Archaeology in Ancient Israel and Beyond*, eds. Assaf Yasur-Landau, Jennie R. Ebeling, and Laura B. Mazow (Leiden: Brill, 2011), 275.

[154] Gil Karie, "A New Silicon Valley in the Middle East," *Forbes International*, October 7, 2015: https://www.forbes.com/sites/forbesinternational/2015/10/07/a-new-silicon-valley-in-the-middle-east/#2e92a704d2b7.

Beersheba, can be hot and dry. You need water if you are going to live in the desert.

The Return to Beersheba

Isaac returns to Beersheba after many years. He is still in Palestine, where God told him to stay, but he has now moved back into the Negev. The famine had lasted several years. He could now return to the place he knew so well. The gentle rains had resumed, the desert wadis (streams) were flowing, and the land once again bloomed with color. But a return to his boyhood home was beset with uncertainty. Isaac had experienced the blessing of God while he was away. He had enjoyed even greater success than his father. He had become wealthy during the famine. He now had a growing family, a large retinue of servants, flocks and herds, and a collection of possessions that likely required a caravan of camels for transport. His return to Beersheba would attract attention. The long line of "desert ships" (camels), as they came to be known, would be seen for miles away. His presence might incite old rivalries. His accomplishments could arouse jealousies. Life had already taught him some hard lessons about fights breaking out in places of flourishing. Abimelech had ordered him to leave Gerar. He still remembered that place he named *Injustice* and the well he called *Adversary*. He had bad memories. But God had also been good to him and had given him *Room* to flourish. What would his return to Beersheba have in store? He might be putting his wife, or children, or servants—maybe everything—in danger. There was no guarantee of safety, success or shalom. And so God appears to him

77

during his move and says, "I am the God of our father Abraham. Do not be afraid, for I am with you; I will bless you and will increase the number of your descendants for the sake of my servant Abraham." God appears to Isaac to calm his fears.

The Peacemaker

Do not be afraid. I am with you. I will bless you. Read those words again and reflect on them. This story and these words were written down for our instruction and encouragement so that we, as the children of Abraham, Isaac and Jacob, would persevere in hope! Yes, you have been through difficult times, and yes, you still live in a dangerous world. But do not be afraid! *Do not be afraid!* Why? God is with you. God Almighty, Creator of heaven and earth, the God of Abraham—is with you! We do not worship a regional deity—one who is confined to one town or city or state or nation. He is present with us wherever we go and whatever we go through. Blessing, as we have said, is not to be confined to the fertile valley of the Nile or a hole in the ground in Gerar; it is found wherever God leads us. We can even flourish in the desert. We can succeed in times of famine. God reassures Isaac that just as he blessed Abraham wherever he went—from Ur to Canaan to Egypt to Beersheba—he would also bless Isaac wherever he went. He would bless his descendants— you and me and all who love him and are called to be his children. Do not fear. He is with you. He will bless you.

Isaac responded to these words in faith. He built an altar to mark this place where God met him, to remember his promise and to bow in worship to God. And then his servants began digging for water.

Just as Isaac was leaving his new "place of worship," Abimelech arrived with his personal advisor and the commander of his forces. One can only imagine what was going through his mind. I would be thinking, *This guy just won't leave my family alone, and I may have to settle this some other way!* It was a calculated move on the part of Abimelech, a cloak and dagger visit, and Isaac knew it. On the one hand, Abimelech was there for diplomacy with his most trusted advisor. But he also traveled with the commander of his forces, who sat as a quiet reminder that Abimelech was a man of power. He was making a statement. Isaac was not happy to see him: "Why have you come to me, since you were hostile to me and sent me away?" [155] As Wenham comments: "Isaac's experiences in Gerar have not been happy, and he bristles with suspicion as he greets them." [156] This is a very normal human response. It explains why Isaac's son, Jacob, fled from Laban and why he avoided his brother Esau even after they had reconciled. It also helps us make sense of Joseph's initial reluctance to let his own brothers back in his life, resorting to unusual methods for testing their hearts. We can all relate to what Isaac must have been feeling when Abimelech arrived with his advisor and commander. I usually find myself caught in between the advice of Jesus, the Son of Sirach in Ecclesiasticus (Sirach), who said, "Never trust

[155] Gen. 26:27.

[156] Wenham, *Genesis 16–50*, 193.

your enemy," [157] and the words of Jesus the Son of David, who told us to "love our enemies." [158] I will confess, I'm usually somewhere in the middle, not trusting my enemies while trying to love them. May God give me grace!

Abimelech presses his case with masterful diplomacy. His words are probably intended to flatter, even if there is truth in them. "We saw clearly that the Lord was with you." [159] "Let us make a treaty with you that you will do us no harm." [160] This is much closer to the real reason for the king's visit. Isaac has become a force to be reckoned with; he is forming new allies and new allegiances. His regional influence is likely growing. Abimelech would not have pursued peace if he did not have some doubt about the trouble Isaac could cause him down the road. The king glosses over the past as though his memory has faded with time. We "did not harm you but always treated you well and sent you away peacefully. And now you are blessed by the Lord." [161] Here was a highly selective recounting of the past. Abimelech had done some good things for Isaac and had commanded others not to hurt him after the wife-sister debacle. But Abimelech had not always treated Isaac well, nor was he blessed by God because of anything the king had done.

---

[157] Ecc. 12:10.

[158] Matt. 5:44.

[159] Gen. 26:28.

[160] Gen. 26:29.

[161] Ibid.

Isaac, who was less than welcoming when the king arrived, softens. He agrees to make peace. Abimelech is not motivated by his desire to do what is right, but by a desire to protect his own power. He perceives that the person he has wronged could become a problem down the road if he continues to make friends with Egyptians and Hittites in the region. Isaac was not naïve, and his willingness to make peace should not be construed as weakness. It is likely due to what we have already learned about Isaac's life—he is a person who prefers peace—and God was bringing peace to him. It had eluded him in the past, but here it was literally chasing after him. Abimelech, who had hounded him in the past, was now in town to make peace. Isaac sees in Abimelech's gesture, whatever the motivation, another sign of God's blessing. The king's arrival had come immediately after God appeared to him in a dream and said, "Don't be afraid, for I am with you: I will bless you." Abimelech's willingness to make peace was another blessing from God. Isaac had tried but failed to make peace in the past. Now God was finally blessing him what he could not achieve on his own. As one commentator observes: "The treaty between Isaac and the Philistines brought a happy resolution to years of dissension."[162] Isaac accepts this as the goodness of God.

A feast is prepared. Isaac and Abimelech eat and drink together. They raise their glasses. They celebrate and mark this special occasion as the people in Palestine did—by breaking bread together. The following

---

[162] Wenham, *Genesis 16–50*, 192.

morning Isaac sends Abimelech, Ahuzzah and Phicol on their way in peace. And then, on that very same day, while Abimelech, his counselor and his commander are riding back to the ancient city of Gerar, Isaac hears the shouting of his servants: "We've found water!" He names the well Shibah, a Hebrew word that means "to swear an oath" or "make a promise."[163] This was the place where God gave Isaac peace through an oath between him and Abimelech. And so he cried out in joy, *Shibah!* And they named the town Beersheba, which means "The Well of the Promise." The God who promised to bless him kept his promise. And this time the Well Digger was blessed with prosperity *and* peace.

---

[163] Brown, Driver and Briggs, *A Hebrew and English Lexicon*, 989.

6

Advice on Well Digging

"Your task is to dig wells in your desert."[164]
——Eugene Peterson

I am writing this little book at the beginning of my sixth decade on this earth. I have moved a lot during the past half-century—a lot more than I would have liked. I was born in Texas City, Texas, in 1967. As a boy, I remember loving the Houston Astros, smoked BBQ brisket, sweet Texas peaches, homemade pecan pie and Blue Bell ice cream. I also fell in love with the wild beauty of Central Texas. In 1975, our family moved to Tennessee, where my dad attended Bible college to prepare for the ministry. In 1979, we moved to Indiana so that dad could further his education. We moved to Kansas in 1981 for dad's first full-time ministry assignment. After a cold winter in Kansas and painful resignation, we moved to Oklahoma for a few months, before returning to Indiana in 1982.

Back in Indiana in 1983, I began dating my high school sweetheart. We were married in 1988, and I became a pastor just a few months later at the age of twenty-one (*What was I thinking?*). Stacy and I had three

---

[164] Eugene H. Peterson, *Subversive Spirituality* (Grand Rapids, MI/Cambridge, UK: Eerdmans, 1997), 39.

boys together—all born in the same small town in Indiana. We served two congregations in the Hoosier state, one for nine years and another for more than twenty years. Then, in 2019, my wife and I moved again, this time to Austin, Texas. It seems poetic in a way, returning to the state where I was born, but to be honest, very little of it was planned in advance! I find that I'm still in love with all those things I remember enjoying as a boy. In fact, I just returned to my study after a long drive with my wife in the hill country outside of Austin. We stopped for a bit in an old Texas town, had a chopped brisket sandwich, and shared some Blue Bell ice cream. I felt like I was a little boy again! Some of my moves have been unwelcome, and nearly all have been unexpected. And yet I can truly say that the Lord has been with me through every bit of it— and blessed me in ways I could not have foreseen. I first read Eugene Peterson's quote about digging wells in your own desert when I was a younger pastor in Indiana. I remember that it strengthened me to work hard right where God had moved me trusting him to bless the work of my hands. I've learned a few things over the years about being a Well Digger, so in these final pages I want to share a few words of encouragement.

Never Give Up—You Are Not Alone

Don't quit! If you have been through a season of loss—whether you have lost a business, a job, a friend, a home, or a relative—it is important to find encouragement from the faithful lives of others. Maybe your loss came during the pandemic or had nothing to do with the season we are living through as I write these words. Hebrews was written to encourage people who were thinking about giving up. The writer urges the followers of Jesus not to give up hope, but to "run with perseverance the race that is marked out for us."[165] We are commanded to fix our eyes on Jesus in this race, and we are also told to find strength in the "great cloud of witnesses" who have finished well.[166] The imagery the writer evokes is that of a running a race in a Roman amphitheater. This was something to which first-century readers could relate. They went to sporting events for recreation, just like we do today. The Greek word translated "cloud" is being used figuratively to convey the idea of "numberless throng," perhaps something akin to our phrase, "a sea of people."[167] This turn of phrase would have evoked the image of a large coliseum filled with a throng of onlookers who had already finished the race and were now sitting in the stands watching you finish yours! As we run this race called life, we can find encouragement from the reality that others have finished strong even through many dangers, toils and snares.[168]

---

[165] Heb. 12:1.

[166] Heb. 12:1–3.

[167] Walter Bauer, William F. Arndt and F. Wilbur Gingrich, *A Greek-English Lexicon of the New Testament and Other Early Christian Literature* (Chicago, IL: University of Chicago Press, 1979), 537.

[168] F. F. Bruce, *The Epistle to the Hebrews* (Grand Rapids, MI: Eerdmans, 1990), 332–41.

There are millions of people in the stands who have finished well. It is a far greater audience than we could possibly imagine. Abraham, Isaac and Jacob. Joseph, Moses, and the people of Israel who "passed through the Red Sea on dry land." The prostitute Rahab is watching and is counted among the faithful! Gideon, Barak, Samson, Jephthah—those who lived in the dark days of the judges. David and Solomon and the kings of Israel surround us, witnesses to the faithfulness of God. The lives of the prophets encourage us. Some of these witnesses escaped the sword, while others were put to death by it. They "conquered kingdoms," and they were also destitute, persecuted and mistreated. They lived by faith. They lived strong. They persevered to the very end in all kinds of circumstances. Their lives are meant to encourage us.[169]

Hebrews 11 is not an exhaustive list of the people of faith. It is, in fact, more like a vignette, giving us a small glimpse into the many faces of faithful people we can look to on this long obedience in the same direction. It's only one chapter of abbreviated faithfulness; there are many stories. I would encourage you to meditate on the lives of people who have been through difficult experiences in their lives and find encouragement from them. This is one way of reminding yourself that you are not alone. I have found encouragement from the life of Isaac and other biblical figures who have faced difficulties and remained faithful. I have also been encouraged by the lives of faithful Christian leaders like

---

[169] Heb. 11:29–38.

Augustine of Hippo, Martin Luther, John Calvin, Jonathan Edwards and C. S. Lewis. We often crib their quotes, but their grit and grace during struggle, depression, rejection and loss is even more inspiring. The biographies of their lives have offered me as much encouragement as the words they have written. Contemporary examples abound of people who are still in the race despite setbacks and suffering. Look around you. Find inspiration in the lives of saints who have finished and those around you who are still running hard. A coach loses his dream job, but he keeps coaching; a public servant loses his election, but finds a place to serve; a wife loses her husband, but learns to live with joy; a child prodigy loses her way, but finds another. Those who have lived before us can inspire us, but those who are still in the race can encourage us to persevere right now! [170] As Winston Churchill has reminded us through his life and by his words: "Never give in. Never give in. *Never, never, never, never*—in nothing, great or small, large or petty—never give in, except to convictions of honour and good sense."[171] Isaac lived through famine, failure, frustration and foe. But he never gave up. He just kept digging wells. And he flourished. You are not alone!

---

[170] Heb. 3:13.

[171] Winston Churchill, as cited in William Manchester and Paul Reid, *The Last Lion: Winston Spencer Churchill Defender of the Realm 1940–1965* (New York, NY: Little, Brown and Company, 2012), 592.

Listen to the Voice of God

It's hard to know what God wants us to do during famine and frustration. We are told not to give up, but what does God want us to do instead? I have discovered that God speaks and works in all kinds of ways. There are some Christian thinkers who believe that decision-making and the will of God really come down to making wise decisions. Weigh the pros and cons, seek godly counsel, and choose from any number of good options. Only after the fact can you say that you are doing the will of God.[172] Others take a more mystical path, believing that God works in subjective ways. They would encourage us to be sensitive to the voice of God. We need to "hear when God is speaking" and "identify a direction he is taking in your life."[173] So do we follow the way of wisdom or the way of wonder? I have turned this question over and over in my mind. And I have now concluded that the answer is *Yes!*

As I read Scripture, and this story is but one illustration, I find encouragement for believers to be as wise as they possibly can while *also* listening to the mysterious voice of God. I understand that there is a difference between descriptive and prescriptive language. Still, I'm not comfortable just dismissing some of what I read in the Scriptures as part of another "dispensation." I find too many instances of God working in mysterious ways in both the Old and New

---

[172] Garry Friesen, *Decision Making and the Will of God* (Sisters, OR: Multnomah, 2004).

[173] Henry Blackaby, *Experiencing God* (Nashville, TN: B&H Publishing, 2003), 5.

Testaments, over the past two thousand years of church history, and now (in an even more convincing way) in the lived experiences of the non-Western Church, which now comprises nearly seventy percent of the word's Christians.

My own views have evolved on this question. Much earlier in my life, I held to a more mystical understanding of the way God led his people, trying to discern that "still small voice" in order to get a sense of what God may be saying to me. It is during difficult times that we most need to hear from God, and I leaned heavily on the subjective aspects of God's work in my heart. I viewed God's work in my life in a mysterious way. In time I became convinced that this approach was fraught with problems and pitfalls. Feelings and intuitions can be dangerous things. In fact, I often "feel" like doing things that could really bring me a lot of pain and suffering at the end of the day. And I don't always "feel" like doing what God clearly commands me to do—like loving my enemies. I needed a better method. And so I came to see the wisdom of the way of wisdom! When I needed to make important decisions, I immersed myself in Scripture, I prayed for wisdom, I sought godly counsel, I weighed various options, and then I did my very best to make good decisions. I moved away from mystery and embraced wisdom. I have now come to the place where I think this was a false dichotomy—an unnecessary and unhelpful "either/or" that I really never lived out consistently. I prefer thinking in terms of method and mystery, or wisdom and wonder.

I believe that Scripture clearly teaches us to be as wise as we can be, while also telling us to leave room for wonder. There are practices in God's word that are commanded—things we should do methodically—pray for wisdom, read the Scriptures, seek good counsel. But there is also some mystery to the way God works in our lives. I have come to believe that living this life well requires living as wisely as we possibly can, while also remaining sensitive to hearing God speak to us in unexpected ways. This happened to me recently.

After thirty years of pastoral ministry, I stepped away from leading a congregation I loved with all my heart. It was my plan to stay for the rest of my life. Following my resignation, I struggled with the question of what God had for me next. I needed good counsel from people who had been through this before. I was shown by experienced guides that I needed a season of lament, time for prayer and space for reflection. I was also advised to rest my mind and body and rely on others to help me find the right vocation. I had become a full-time pastor at the age of twenty-one—much younger than the average minister. During the course of more than thirty years, I led two congregations, earned three graduate degrees (including a very rigorous Ph.D.), prepared and delivered hundreds of sermons, traveled extensively for mission work, taught theology overseas, helped raise ministry funds, guided both churches through multiple building projects, worked with boards and committees, mentored and managed staff members, performed weddings, conducted funerals, provided pastoral care and tried my best to keep up with all the stuff that church-growth experts were saying. Every pastor who has ever led a church knows how easy it is to take on too much—and I often did. Still, I loved it, and leaving was hard.

In my case, I wanted to be sure I wasn't just listening to the opinion of only one person. So I sought out several sensible people—all of whom were experienced and wise advisors. I reflected carefully on their counsel and followed the professional advice I was given. I rested. I slept in for the first time in my life—getting up around seven o'clock every morning (I used to begin my day at 5 am). I read good books without needing to think about writing sermons. It felt like a vacation every day, even though I was still hurting. I spent time with my wife, went to see my parents and kids, and whiled away several weeks in Cambridge with good books and good coffee and good ale! I grieved—I spent time with a spiritual director and poured out my pain and asked my questions and talked about all the things that were going on in my heart. I also talked with people who were skilled at helping people like me discover the right opportunities. I applied to university posts and interviewed for some really amazing jobs. I almost became a professor—it seemed like a perfect job. But I didn't want to leave ministry—yet. I talked with several churches—some large and wealthy—others smaller and more modest. Perhaps a different setting would be more conducive to the way God had made me.

And then came an unexpected text from a friend who said he wanted me to meet someone for coffee. The person he wanted me to talk to was leading an organization that was equipping pastors in the developing world. They were looking for an experienced pastor with a strong academic background who knew his way around the globe and had a passion for equipping pastors and ministry leaders. *What?* I had followed the way of wisdom, but this was like *Wow!* It was totally unexpected. I called and apologized to the recruiter I was working with right after a weekend interview and said I needed to put everything else on hold. A few days later, my wife and I were on a flight to Montana, where I interviewed for my current position. I still remember sitting outside next to Rock Creek at a board member's home a stone's throw from Yellowstone National Park. My wife was next to me, the board members were seated outside in a circle on a beautiful fall afternoon, and I just had this sense that God was doing something that I couldn't put into words. I was overwhelmed with emotion—not only by the beauty of what looked like a scene out of the movie *A River Runs Through It*, but also by the sense that God was working in some mysterious way. He was speaking.

How can I discount the mysterious ways of God? I have read about His ways in Scripture, I have heard the inspirational confessions of his saints, and I have experienced his workings in my own life. So this is my best pastoral counsel: When you are not sure what to do in times of famine or failure or frustration, read the Scriptures, pray for wisdom, seek godly counsel, invite people to help you as you consider what to do next— and follow the good advice you are given with all your might. But while you are doing this, listen for the other ways God may speak to you. He speaks in all kinds of ways, through ordinary means and in extraordinary ways. He may just surprise you. I believe in taking the path of wisdom, but I also believe that sometimes God meets us on the path in some wonderful, unexplainable way. Wisdom *and* wonder.

Believe in the Goodness of God

It is difficult to think that God is good when we are going through times that are so bad. This may be one of the reasons God appeared to Abraham, Isaac and Jacob more than once and repeated his promises. You don't need reassurance when everything is going well. You need it when you are living in a famine and when you have just had a frightening experience. The pain that exists in this world can lead people to ask ultimate questions, as it did for the Oxford thinker C. S. Lewis. The problem of suffering can also lead people away from the faith, as it did for theologian and philosopher Bart D. Ehrman.[174] By the grace of God, I have chosen the path of Lewis over Ehrman. But I can sympathize with anyone who struggles with faith in times of pain and suffering.

One of the strongest arguments for the goodness of God, it turns out, is the goodness most of us experience in our lives every day. How could we even begin to put down on paper all the good things we taste and see and smell and touch and hear nearly every day of our lives? This world, and our lives, are dripping with the goodness of God. It is all around us. And we haven't even trotted out the promise of God to bless us through

---

[174] Bart D. Ehrman, God's Problem: How the Bible Fails to Answer Our Most Important Question—Why We Suffer (New York, NY: HarperCollins, 2008), 1–19.

Christ for all eternity! While evil led Ehrman away from God, it paradoxically led C. S. Lewis to God. As Lewis questioned the problem of suffering and evil in the world as an atheist at Oxford, he began to question why he was even asking the question. His conclusion was that his preoccupation with the problem of suffering and evil proved that there was such a thing as goodness and justice, and he had to account for this "belief." Where did he get such a notion to begin with? As such, he found that focusing only on the "problem of evil" was to ignore the "problem of goodness." As he put it:

> My argument against God was that the universe seemed so cruel and unjust. But how had I got this idea of just and unjust? A man does not call a line crooked unless he has some idea of a straight line. Thus in the very act of trying to prove that God did not exist—in other words, that the whole of reality was senseless—I found I was forced to assume that one part of reality—namely my idea of justice—was full of sense. Consequently atheism turns out to be too simple.[175]

This was not Lewis' solution to the problem of suffering and evil in the world—he would address this topic more fully in later works like *The Problem of Pain*.[176] Lewis was only saying that when ardent unbelievers point to evil in the world as an argument against the existence of God, they are tacitly admitting that there is

---

[175] Lewis, Mere Christianity, 38–9.

[176] Lewis, *The Problem of Pain* (New York, NY: HarperCollins, 2001).

such a thing as goodness in the world, and this also requires a plausible explanation.

I find pain and suffering in this world to be a profound mystery, and I can empathize with every person who doubts in times of difficulty. I can sympathize with Ehrman, an impressive scholar and a person who is created and loved by God. I have doubted. But I cannot get away from the goodness of God. I have read about the goodness of God in Scripture—in what God says about himself—and what he has done for his people. I have heard about God's goodness through the testimonies of sinners and saints. I have tasted and seen the goodness of God in my life again and again—even through the dark valleys. And so, when famine comes, I must remind myself of what I know to be true: God is good, and I will taste and see his goodness again! He has promised to bless his people with his goodness wherever they go. He doesn't just confine his blessing to one hole in the ground in one small town in Canaan. He has blessed me in Texas, and Tennessee, and Indiana, and Kansas and Oklahoma, and Indiana (again)—and now back in Texas![177]

---

[177] Over the course of many years, I have devoted significant time to studying the existential problem of suffering and evil. It first captured my attention during graduate work when I was assigned a paper on the topic, and I have revisited this subject many times. The literature on this topic is immense. One of the more helpful works for me has been D. A. Carson, *The Difficult Doctrine of the Love of God* (Wheaton, IL: Crossway Books, 1999).

Live with All Your Might

My life's mantra is actually one of the resolutions of the American theologian Jonathan Edwards (1703–1758): "Resolved, to live with all my might, while I do live." [178] I always dreamed of being a "settled minister"—an old expression used for an English pastor who devoted his entire life to staying in the same town and serving one congregation his entire life. This, too, was Edwards' dream. And then the most famous pastor in all of New England was "ejected" from his pulpit in Northampton. It was a trying experience, and he worried most about his family. He wrote about his dreadful experience in his journals and other writings. But he stayed true to his resolution to live strong. He became a pastor to American Indians in Stockbridge, took up his pen and wrote inspiring theological treatises (that we are still reading!) and then became president of Princeton before his death. [179] Edwards faced disappointments, but he continued to live with all his might.

When I was unexpectedly unsettled, it was very difficult for me. And when I took on a new role, I was ready to work, but I wasn't quite ready to open my life up to meaningful relationships. I still remember a board member saying to me not long after I accepted my new position, "Hey, I really want to fly you and your wife

---

[178] Jonathan Edwards, *Jonathan Edwards' Resolutions: And Advice to Young Converts*, ed. Stephen J. Nichols (Philipsburg, PA: P&R Publishers, 2001), 3.

[179] George Marsden, *Jonathan Edwards: A Life* (New Haven, MA: Yale University Press, 2003), 341–394,

down to Central America—we've got a beautiful place. We'd love to just hang out." I remember thinking, *I don't really want any friends right now—that will be a 'no' for now. I just want to do my job.* I'm smiling as I write this—because this particular man has become a very good friend, and I plan to be with him in another beautiful place in just a few weeks (and yes—we've taken him up on his offer more than once now!). For me, digging new wells means a lot of things. It means saying yes to invitations from colleagues to do fun things together. It certainly means rolling up my sleeves and working hard and smart for the organization I serve. It means loving the staff members I work with, leading them well, finding joy in their successes and even laughing with them. It means opening my life up to some amazing relationships in my work and travel. It means becoming immersed in a new church community, joining a men's group in Austin and exploring new ways to serve the local church in the United States. It means working with leaders in Africa, Asia and Latin America—those who are getting it done in the "hard places." It means being present—physically and emotionally—with my family. I'm digging new wells.

What does digging new wells look like for you? Does it mean starting a new career and just going for it with all your might, even though you are afraid? Does it mean saying yes to invitations to hang out with new friends, even though you are still hurting from the past? Does it mean getting involved in a new local community with all that comes with it—a new doctor, a new dentist, a new lawyer, a new school, a new neighborhood? It's not always easy, but it can be an adventure! Does it mean starting a new degree program, even later in life, just because you've always wanted to? What is God saying to you through this little book? Don't be afraid. He is with you. He will bless you. Dig some new wells!

And remember that you are not really starting over. Isaac took his well-digging skills with him everywhere he went. There is certainly something to be said for this. If God has moved you to another place in life, you may feel like you are starting over, but you really aren't. You are bringing with you many years (in some cases, many decades) of accumulated God-given experiences that will help you in your new place. I'm a very different person now than I was in my early twenties, and I'm using all the things I have learned over the last few decades in my new vocation. And I'm also learning more new things. I'm sure Isaac learned with every move and every mistake and every man-made hole he put in the ground.

But we must remember that Isaac prospered because of God's blessing. He tucked in his tunic and tore into the earth, but God guided him to the right places and caused the desert to bloom. We must work with all our might! Recall the words of the Teacher: "Whatever your hand finds to do, do it with all your might."[180] And then we must put our trust in a God who has promised to bless us. We work, and then we pray: "May the favor of the Lord our God rest on us: establish the work of our hands for us—yes, establish the work of our hands." Our hands may dig wells, but we need God to bless the

---

[180] Ecc. 9:10.

work of our hands. So go for it. Life is short; live it to the fullest. *Carpe diem*! Dig wells in your desert.

Select Bibliography

Alkire, S., R. Nogales, N. N. Quinn and N. Suppa. "On
    Track or Not? Projecting the Global Multidimensional
    Poverty Index." OPHI Research in Progress, 58a.
    University of Oxford, 2020.

Arnold, Bill T. *Genesis*. Cambridge, UK: Cambridge
    University Press, 2014.

Augustine of Hippo. *The Confessions*. Edited by Philip Burton.
    New York, NY: Random House, 2001.

Bauer, Walter, William F. Arndt and Wilbur Gingrich. *A
    Greek-English Lexicon of the New Testament and Other Early
    Christian Literature*. Chicago, IL: Chicago University
    Press, 1979.

Bar, Shaul. *Isaac: The Passive Patriarch*. Eugene, OR: Wipf &
    Stock, 2019.

Blackaby, Henry. *Experiencing God*. Nashville, TN: B&H
    Publishing, 2005.

Boice, James Montgomery. *Genesis. An Expositional Commentary*.
    Volume 2. Grand Rapids, MI: Eerdman, 1985.

Bowler, Kate. *Blessed: A History of the American Prosperity Gospel*.
    New York, NY: Oxford University Press, 2013.

Brown, Francis, S. R. Driver and Charles A. Briggs. *A Hebrew and English Lexicon of the Old Testament*. Oxford, UK: Oxford University Press, 1951.

Bruce, F. F. *The Epistle to the Hebrews*. Grand Rapids, MI: Eerdmans, 1990.

Bunyan, John. *The Pilgrim's Progress: from this World to That which is to Come*. Edited by James Blanton Wharey and Roger Sharrock. Oxford, UK: Oxford University Press, 1967.

Burroughs, Augsten. *Dry: A Memoir*. New York, NY: St. Martin's Press, 2013.

Calvin, John. *Commentaries on the Book of Moses Called Genesis*. Volume 1. Grand Rapids, MI: Baker Book House, 1998.

————. *Institutes of the Christian Religion*. In *The Library of Christian Classics*. Vol. 20. Edited by John T. McNeill. Philadelphia, PA: The Westminster Press, 1960.

Camus, Albert. *The Plague*. New York, NY: Vintage, 1991.

Carson, D. A. *The Difficult Doctrine of the Love of God*. Wheaton, IL: Crossway Books, 1999.

Chesterton, G. K. *Orthodoxy*. London, UK: John Lane, 1908.

Edgar, William. "The Creation Mandate." *The Gospel Coalition*. August 25, 2020: https://www.thegospelcoalition.org/essay/the-creation-mandate/.

Edwards, Jonathan. *Jonathan Edward's Resolutions: And Advice to Young Converts*. Edited by Stephen J. Nichols. Philipsburg, PA: P&R Publishers, 2001.

Ehrman, Bart D. *God's Problem: How the Bible Fails to Answer Our Most Important Question—Why We Suffer*. New York, NY: HarperCollins, 2008.

Erickson, Millard J. *Christian Theology*. Grand Rapids, MI: Baker Book House, 1985.

Ewing, W. and D. J. Wend. "Jacob's Well." In *The International Bible Encyclopedia*. Edited by Geoffrey W. Bromiley. Grand Rapids, MI: Eerdmans, 1982.

Feinberg, John S. "Evil, the Problem of." In *Evangelical Dictionary of Theology*. Edited by Walter E. Elwell. Grand Rapids, MI: Baker, 1984.

Feinberg, John S., ed. *Continuity and Discontinuity: Perspectives on the Relationship Between the Old and New Testaments*. Westchester, IL: Crossway Books, 1988.

Friesen, Garry. *Decision Making and the Will of God*. Sisters, OR: Multnomah, 2004.

Bibliography

Hamilton, Victor P. *The Book of Genesis, Chapters 18–50.* Grand Rapids, MI: Eerdmans, 1995. https://www.biblicalarchaeology.org/scholars-study/tunnel/.

"Hezekiah's Tunnel." *Biblical Archaeology Society*, August 13, 2013: https://www.biblicalarchaeology.org/scholars-study/tunnel/.

Jenkins, Philip. *The New Faces of Christianity: Believing the Bible in the Global South.* Oxford, UK: Oxford University Press, 2006.

Karie, Gil. "A New Silicon Valley in the Middle East." *Forbes International.* October 7, 2015: https://www.forbes.com/sites/forbesinternational/2015/10/07/a-new-silicon-valley-in-the-middle-east/#2e92a704d2b7.

Kidner, Derek. *Genesis: An Introduction and Commentary.* Leicester, UK: Inter-Varsity Press, 1967.

Knight III, George W. "The Scriptures Were Written for Our Instruction." *Journal of the Evangelical Theological Society.* Vol. 39, No. 1. March 1996: 3–13.

Lewis, C. S. *The Problem of Pain.* New York. NY: HarperCollins, 2001.

————. *Mere Christianity.* New York, NY: HarperCollins, 2001.

Luther, Martin. *Lectures on Romans*. Edited by William Pauck. Louisville, KY: John Knox Press, 1961.

Malamat, A. "Aspects of the Foreign Policy of David and Solomon." *Journal of Near Eastern Studies*. Vol. 22. No. 1 (January 1963): 1–17.

Manchester, William and Paul Reid, *The Last Lion: Winston Spencer Churchill Defender of the Realm 1940–1965*. New York, NY: Little, Brown and Company, 2012.

Mangum, R. Todd. and Mark S. Sweetnam. *The Scofield Reference Bible: Its History and Impact on the Evangelical Church*. Colorado Springs, CO: Paternoster, 2009.

Manning, Brennan. *The Ragamuffin Gospel*. Colorado Springs, CO: Multnomah Books, 2005.

Marsden, George. *Jonathan Edwards: A Life*. New Haven, MA: Yale University Press, 2003.

Matthews, Victor H. "The Wells of Gerar." *The Biblical Archaeologist*. Vol. 49, No. 2 (June 1986): 118–26.

McGrath, Alister E. *IUSTITIA DEI: A History of the Doctrine of Justification*. Cambridge, UK: Cambridge University Press, 1998.

McDermott, Gerald R. *The New Christian Zionism: Fresh Perspectives on Israel and the Land.* Downers Grove, IL: IVP Academic, 2016.

Origen. *Homilies on Genesis and Exodus.* Translated by Robert E. Heine. Washington, D.C.: The Catholic University Press of America, 1981.

Oxfam Media Briefing, "The Hunger Virus: How COVID-10 is Fuelling Hunger in a Hungry World." July 9, 2020: https://oxfamilibrary.openrepository.com/bitstream/handle/10546/621023/mb-the-hunger-virus-090720-en.pdf.

Peterson, Eugene H. *A Long Obedience in the Same Direction.* Downers Grove, IL: InterVarsity Press, 2019.

———. *Subversive Spirituality.* Grand Rapids, MI/Cambridge, UK: Eerdmans, 1997.

Poythress, Vern S. *Understand Dispensationalists.* Phillipsburg, NJ: P&R Publishing, 1986.

Roop, Eugene F. *Genesis: Believer's Bible Commentary.* Scottdale, PA: Herald Press, 1977.

Schulman, Alan R. "Diplomatic Marriage in the Egyptian New Kingdom." *Journal of Near Eastern Studies.* Vol. 38. No. 3. (July 1979): 177–93.

Bibliography

Singer-Avitz, Lily. "Household Activities At Tel Beersheba."
In *Household Archaeology in Ancient Israel and Beyond*. Edited
by Assaf Yasur-Landau, Jennie R. Ebeling and Laura B.
Mazow. Leiden: Brill, 2011.

Sneh, Amihai, Ram Weinberger and Eyal Shalev, "The
Why, How, and When of the Siloam Tunnel Re-
evaluated." *The Bulletin of American Schools of Oriental
Research*. No. 359 (August 2010): 57–65.

UNESCO. World Heritage List. "Biblical Tels—Megiddo,
Hazor, Beer Sheba":
https://whc.unesco.org/en/list/1108.

Waltke, Bruce. *Genesis: A Commentary*. Grand Rapids, MI:
Zondervan, 2001.

Walton, John H. and D. Brent Sandy, *The Lost World of
Scripture: Ancient Literary Culture and Biblical Authority*.
Downers Grove, IL: IVP Academic, 2013.

Wenham, Gordon. *Word Biblical Commentary, Genesis 16–50*.
Nashville, TN: Thomas Nelson Publishers, 1994.

Wright, N. T. *God and the Pandemic: A Christian Reflection on the
Coronavirus and Its Aftermath*. Grand Rapids, MI:
Zondervan, 2020

Contact Information

United States and Canada

F. Lionel Young III
Global Action
PO Box 117
Wheaton, IL 60187
www.globalaction.com

United Kingdom

F. Lionel Young
Cambridge Centre for Christianity Worldwide
Westminster College
Madingley Road
Cambridge, UK
CB3 0AA
https://www.cccw.cam.ac.uk/

F. Lionel Young III is a Research Associate at the Cambridge Centre for Christianity Worldwide in Cambridge, England and the Executive Vice President of Global Action. He holds a PhD from the University of Stirling (Scotland) where he was mentored by the British intellectual David W. Bebbington. Lionel also holds Masters degrees in theology and church history from Trinity Evangelical Divinity School and Grace Theological Seminary. He credits another British thinker, C. S. Lewis, for his love of good books and British ale. Lionel's academic work in the history of Christianity and his research and travels in Africa, Asia and Latin America have deeply influenced his understanding of Scripture. When he is not hidden away in an old library in Cambridge, he is teaching pastors and ministry leaders in the non-Western world. He and his wife Stacy make their home in Austin, Texas.

www.ingramcontent.com/pod-product-compliance
Lightning Source LLC
LaVergne TN
LVHW041230080426
835508LV00011B/1138

* 9 7 8 0 5 7 8 7 7 5 4 7 0 *